SEASONS OF THE JOURNEY
THE BIOGRAPHY OF
DR. JAMES FRANK

SEASONS OF THE JOURNEY
THE BIOGRAPHY OF
DR. JAMES FRANK

Trailblazer, Leader, & Legend

Dr. Zelma Lloyd Frank

JAMEZELL PARTNERS PRESS
Atlanta, Georgia

SEASONS OF THE JOURNEY
THE BIOGRAPHY OF
DR. JAMES FRANK

Trailblazer, Leader & Legend

Published by Jamezell Partners Press
Atlanta, Georgia
jamezellpress@gmail.com

Trent Frank, Editorial Director and Contributor
Troy Frank, Photo and Content Editor, and Contributor
Yvonne Rose/Quality Press.info, Book Packager

Cover Photo:
The photograph was taken while Commissioner
of the Southwestern Athletic Conference (SWAC)

Copyright © 2023 by Dr. Zelma Lloyd Frank
Paperback ISBN #: 979-8-9881321-0-3
Hardcover ISBN #: 979-8-9881321-3-4
Ebook ISBN #: 979-8-9881321-2-7
Library of Congress Control Number: 2023906568

Dedication

This book is dedicated to the memory of my husband of sixty years, Dr. James Frank, whose stupendous journey I am blessed and privileged to have the opportunity to record in this biography. Also, I dedicate this book to my sons, Trent and Troy, who have their own storied journeys, and to my grandchildren, Tracia and Simeon, whose journeys have only just begun. Finally, I dedicate this work to all of our family and friends whose journeys have at some point in time interfaced, crossed, mingled, and somehow impacted our journey.

Author's Note

The author completed the first draft of this biography before Dr. Frank's passing, so he had read it and penned his concluding notes found at the end of this biography. Ultimately, the need to change the verb tense in the text from present to past was a very challenging and deeply emotional transition for the writer to contemplate.

Acknowledgments

I want to acknowledge those persons who played a role in the compilation, writing, research, and/or editing of this biography.

First, I give honor to God for making it all possible.

I thank my husband, Dr. James Frank, for his input and cooperation, although, in his great humility, he was never fully convinced that I should even write his story. Nevertheless, without his permission, insight, suggestions, patiently answering my many questions, and editing for factual and emotional accuracy, completing this biography would not have been accomplished. Moreover, his mere presence during this process was indescribably supportive and reassuring.

I am humbly and deeply appreciative that Dr. Mark Emmert, NCAA president, graciously honored my request to write the Forward to this biography. On numerous occasions, through his spoken and written words and actions, he has shown in-depth knowledge, understanding, and appreciation for Dr. Frank and his unprecedented contributions to the world of intercollegiate athletics and higher education. He has helped keep Dr. Frank's legacy alive.

With deep gratitude, I acknowledge and appreciate Dr. Charles McClelland, SWAC Commissioner, for his supportive spirit and response to my request for written information. In his current role, and as one who knew and greatly respected Dr. Frank, his contributions have been crucial.

Thanks to Mr. Mark Schleer, the archivist at Lincoln University, and Ms. Ithaca Bryant, assistant to the archivist. I so deeply appreciate their swift and thorough responses to all of my requests for information. I acknowledge their diligence as archivists. They knew Dr. Frank personally, have written about him, and have proudly supervised and promoted the preservation of his history.

I am indebted to my late sister, Mrs. Juanella Bradley, a longtime educator whose connectivity, enthusiasm, feedback, and editorial suggestions were timely, insightful, and invaluable.

I offer posthumous thanks to my late friend, Mrs. Mabelle Thompson, a long-time educator and former colleague who slowly and methodically read the first draft of the manuscript and offered many prudent suggestions. Her sense of humor was also timely and very helpful.

I recognize with gratitude my long-time friend and former colleague, Dr. Theresa DeGruy, college administrator/mental health professional, for her unwavering support and encouragement, and assistance in electronically sending the initial draft of the manuscript to the publisher.

I treasure the contributions of my niece, Dr. Stacia Bradley Brown, a retired educator, who guided me in solving some technical issues, gave encouraging commentary, and kept a commitment to attend a writing seminar with me. She also edited one of the drafts.

My appreciation goes out to Dr. Dennis Kimbro, motivational speaker, and bestselling author. He very readily has given concrete and meaningful consultation regarding the nuances of editing, publication options, and other procedural matters. He has been a much-needed source of wisdom and guidance.

I appreciate NCAA Assistant Director of Executive Affairs, Michael Cioroianu for his prompt response to my request for specific pictures in the NCAA Archives. His assistance and enthusiasm have played an essential role in this process.

Thanks to Mrs. Yvonne Rose, director, Quality Press. Her editing, suggestions, patience, understanding, encouragement, and timely responses have been indispensable and greatly appreciated.

It is with the deepest gratitude that I acknowledge Mrs. Barbara Lee Johnson, retired English teacher. Her thorough and heartfelt editing of the final draft has made a significant improvement in the presentation of this biography. Also, thanks to my good friend Rev. Dr. Keith Reynolds who referred Ms. Johnson to me.

I acknowledge with gratitude the noteworthy and numerous contributions from my nephew, Mr. Clifton Johnson, financial advisor, founder and CEO of the nonprofit Empower Series organization. His enthusiasm for writing this biography has never wavered and has served as a constant reminder of its necessity. He was diligent in reading and giving feedback on the first draft of the manuscript and electronically submitting photographs, many from his collection. Throughout the process, he has remained on call and has quickly responded to all requests for assistance. Clifton's contributions have mirrored his depth of understanding regarding the historical significance of Dr. Frank's numerous and mammoth contributions to higher education and national intercollegiate sports.

Some of the pictures used in this book were taken at events Clifton scheduled in different states throughout the years for the sole purpose of Dr. Frank's verbal sharing of his knowledge and storied career.

I sincerely appreciate the contributions of my two sons, Rev. Trent Frank, Lieutenant Colonel, US Army, (Ret.), and Dr. Troy Frank, professor in the School of Business at Lincoln University in Missouri. Troy added invaluable insights and information as he thoroughly, slowly, and painstakingly provided subjective and objective input regarding content, format, photo choices, presentation, and publication. He critiqued the accuracy, relevance, and sequence of historical occurrences as he recalled and also experienced some of them as they played out in his father's life. His rich, loving, and in-depth poetic renderings about his father grace the pages of this biography. He has always referred to his father as his "Hero," and understood the depth of his father's immense contributions as reflected in his thorough and insightful suggestions during the process of compiling this manuscript. He suggested, instinctively and unequivocally, that his father be accurately described in the title of the biography as a trailblazer, leader, and legend. As a result, those three words are appropriately used in the title.

Trent has worked on the manuscript tirelessly and unceasingly. As a result, his contributions have been immeasurable. He has thoroughly scrutinized and contributed to every aspect of the manuscript – writing, editing, formatting, layout, photo selection, and presentation. In many instances, he submitted substantive additions and/or changes to the manuscript. He has accurately sequenced history, lists of honors, awards, and recognitions, and he has researched avenues for publication. He set deadlines and kept everyone on task, organized, time-sensitive, and goal-oriented. He completed a tremendous amount of in-depth research, orchestrated the production, and served as "Editor in Chief" through countless revisions while displaying prayerful wisdom, patience, and persistence.

I am indebted to my many friends and relatives who have listened, repeatedly inquired about progress, and have made thoughtful suggestions at appropriate intervals throughout this process. Their interest and support have been extremely inspirational.

Again, I am thankful for God's presence and guidance throughout the process of writing this manuscript.

Table of Contents

Foreword

A Truly Remarkable Man

This is a tale of a truly remarkable man who led a truly remarkable life. James Frank was indeed a man for all seasons. Raised in the hardscrabble steel town of Aliquippa, Pennsylvania, he was not blessed with an obvious route to success and greatness. On the contrary, Frank's story is a reflection of his unyielding willingness to step bravely into the next adventure without guideposts, without maps. And what an adventure it was.

Today, overuse has rendered the phrase "servant leader" a bit trite. But in this story, the expression seems perfectly suited for Frank. Being of service to others was clearly the animating force of his life. Each step in his passage through the seasons was defined by what he could do to support, nurture and develop others, not just himself.

The stories of his youth, college days, time in the military, development as a professional and leadership at the highest levels, and most especially of his roles as a husband and father, point the reader to the singular conclusion that Frank was a man devoted to principle, integrity, and love of those he served. This biography provides us — in fact, it blesses us — with a role model that placed his priorities in the right order, something so many of us articulate, but so few of us achieve.

As readers, we are fortunate to have had a thoughtful and careful author who also just happened to be his loving wife, Zelma Frank. A highly accomplished academic in her own right, she has assembled a biography that is factual rather than boastful — and I am confident James would have liked that — although her pride certainly shines through. Similarly, the role of his sons in this narrative adds a personal touch of honesty and love. You cannot read the book without feeling the connection between the family members and those others who were touched by James Frank.

Many of the achievements of Frank's life have been accomplished by others. There are many who have played college basketball, who have served our nation in uniform, who have earned a doctorate, who have become leaders within their chosen profession, and been model husbands and fathers. It is, however, extraordinarily rare to find someone who has achieved each of those accomplishments — and indeed many more — in a single lifetime. This story deserves our attention because of that rarity, because James Frank did all those things, and we should all know his story and learn from his example.

Mark A. Emmert
NCAA President

Introduction

Do not follow where the path may lead.
Go instead where there is no path and leave a trail.
Ralph Waldo Emerson

This story is about a man who was intelligent, compassionate, honest, humble, and blessed with a "quiet strength." He accomplished much, including many "firsts." Although having climbed to the top of the mountain in his profession, he never lost the common touch, always remaining level-headed, feet flat on the ground and placed appropriately. He was a man whose story the writer is blessed to have the opportunity to share.

His professional career was expansive and exemplary. He served in many different capacities. The seven usually noted in the literature about him are student-athlete, army lieutenant, college professor, head basketball coach, college president, NCAA President, and commissioner of the Southwestern Athletic Conference (SWAC).

Dr. Frank was the only alumnus of Lincoln University to become president of the institution. He was the first full-time commissioner of the Southwestern Athletic Conference (SWAC). He was the first college president and only African American to become president of the NCAA and had an impactful influence on the incorporation of women's sports into the NCAA hierarchy.

He was instrumental in increasing minority participation in policy decisions and elevating academic eligibility standards and the performance of freshmen athletes. He influenced television contract negotiations and the restructuring of association leadership.

Dr. Frank, a man of humble beginnings, traversed many roads. This biography contains an in-depth view of his personality, character, demeanor, philosophy, and leadership style. His journey, as discussed in this book, will reveal many of the characteristics necessary for successful leadership at the local, regional, and national levels. strength of character, courage, optimism, hard work, perseverance, and creativity - all come into play as the story of this trailblazer, leader, and legend unfolds.

Because he was so effective in his different leadership roles, Dr. Frank was often labeled "A Man for All Seasons." He was a man of many firsts and in some ways an unsung hero. In Chapter eleven, his younger son, Troy, has captured the story of his father's journey in a poem titled, "A Man for All Seasons." His elder son, Trent, has chronicled the essence of his leadership principles. His journey has been recorded in this biography written by his wife, Dr. Zelma Lloyd Frank.

This biography has been written because it is important to record history and mark a legacy. Equally important is the fact that this biography is about a man whose life can serve to inspire and teach others, including those young people who will be our future leaders. To the readers of this book, I invite you to come along with me on this journey through the seasons of Dr. James Frank's life.

Chapter 1

The Journey Begins

There is a time for everything, and a season for every activity under the heavens: a time to be born and a time to die, a time to plant and a time to uproot that which was planted.
Ecclesiastes 3:1-2

Know from whence you came. If you know whence you came there are absolutely no limitations to where you can go.
James Baldwin

It is good to have an end to journey toward, but it is the journey that matters in the end.
Ernest Hemmingway

Dr. James Frank's Parents, Willie & Essie Mae Frank

This story is about an American icon who grew up as a poor child in the hills of Aliquippa, Pennsylvania, a town where the only industry was the manufacturing of steel. The Jones and Laughlin Steel Mill (J & L) in Aliquippa was, at one point, "second in size only to Carnegie Steel."[1] An opportunity for employment in the steel mill drew immigrants from around the world. "They came from Italy, Germany, Russia, Poland, Hungary, Ukraine, Croatia, Serbia, Slovakia, Lebanon, Greece; they were Slavs and Roman Catholics and Jews and Eastern Orthodox."[2]

From Farm to Furnace

Into this milieu also came a multitude of people of African descent from the Southern States in America. Jim Frank's parents, Willie and Essie Mae Glenn Frank, like so many other Blacks during that historical period beginning in the early 1900s that became known as the "Great Migration," moved from the south to find jobs and seek additional opportunities to improve their lives. "Specifically, many Blacks moved to work in the steel industry of western Pennsylvania because of the booming growth in the industry, a Black workforce that had training from southern steel mills, and because of congressional legislation that opened the doors of employment and labor unions for African Americans."[3]

---

[1] S.L. Price, *Playing Through the Whistle: Steel, Football, and an American Town* (New York, Atlantic Monthly Press, 2016), 9.

[2] Price, Playing, 8.

[3] "Black Steelworkers in Western Pennsylvania," Pennsylvania Heritage, last modified December 1977, https://www.paheritage.wpengine.com/article/black-steelworkers-western-pennsylvania/

His parents were from Blakeley, Georgia, where his father had been a farmer. They moved to Aliquippa, Pennsylvania with great anticipation.

His father found work in the blast furnace area of J&L. As recorded in Price's book, "James Frank's father, Willie Frank Sr, began a thirty-year stint as a blast furnace keeper, standing in unmeltable wooden shoes for hours in the breathless heat and opening a chute whenever the molten overflowed."[4] It was a hot, dirty, dangerous job. He worked in the now-defunct steel mill until he retired. After he ceased working in the steel mill, he went into the ministry and became the pastor of a small church in Midland, Pennsylvania. Dr. Frank's maternal grandfather stayed with the family for a short period, and so did his paternal grandfather. Although he could visualize them, being so young, he could not recall any specific interactions with them.

Aliquippa was divided into neighborhoods or sections labeled by numbered plans. The Frank family lived on Wykes Street, in Plan 11. Like most of the properties, the house was owned by the steel mill company and rented to the employee's family. The steel mill deducted rent from the employee's paychecks. That situation brings to mind the words from a former number-one hit song, "Sixteen Tons," sung by Ernie Ford: "Saint Peter don't you call me, 'cause' I can't go, I owe my soul to the company store." Although the song is about a coal miner's life working in a coal mine, the life

---

[4] Price, Playing, 24

experiences were very similar as far as debt to the company- in this case, the steel mill.

Early Photo with Brothers and Parents (from left to right:
Albert, James, Robert, Eddie, Parents, and Willie Jr.)

Willie and Essie Mae Frank, during their adjustment to living in Aliquippa, Pennsylvania, became the parents of five boys, each born two years apart. The firstborn was Eddie. In order of birth, the others were Robert, James, Albert, and Willie.

This story is about James, affectionately called "Jimmy," sometimes "Coach," and, sometimes, "Jim." All of these monikers will be used in this writing based on the season of his life discussed. He earned his doctorate degree at a young age; consequently, Dr. Frank is the title most often used throughout this biography which will chronicle his journey to becoming an American icon. He was the first of his siblings to attend college and the only one to graduate from college. The span of his career included being a high school and college athlete, army officer, university basketball coach, college professor, Dean of Students, Vice President, President, NCAA Secretary-Treasurer, NCAA President, and College Athletics Conference Commissioner. He indeed became "A Man for all Seasons."

Humble Beginnings

On a cold and moonlit night in Aliquippa, Pennsylvania, October 6, 1930, the middle son, James Frank, was born. The writer can only imagine there must have been something about his birth that ignited the atmosphere with spiritual messages and signals that indicated something was different about this newborn child. It must have appeared as if there was an anointing from God. This middle child would take on the best traits of his mother and father. His presence and path seemed ordered by the Lord from the beginning. He entered this world during a time of historical events: the discovery of Pluto, Mahatma Gandhi's 200-mile Salt March, the invention of the jet engine, and the Great Depression.

His early life was filled with school activities, Sunday morning church, and life's usual, sometimes taken-for-granted routine. Sadly, early one morning in February 1942, Dr. Frank's mother, Mrs. Essie Mae Frank, died suddenly. Her youngest son was eight, and the oldest was sixteen.

The landscape changed in many ways when his father was left to raise five boys alone. James, the middle son, was 12 years old when his mother died. He often recalled that his mother's favorite song was the old gospel hymn, "Take My Hand Precious Lord," composed by Dr. Thomas A. Dorsey, an African American musician, evangelist, and composer (1899-1993). Years later, after one other marriage, his father married Lillian Sellers "Mamma Lil," and, to that union, were born three children, Leona "Lee," Rosetta "Zet," and Ronald "Ronnie."

During those years, Jimmy worked hard to help his father make money which was very much needed to maintain a family of five boys. His father bought a small pick-up truck and started a business. Jimmy and his brothers used the truck to haul coal, pick up trash and garbage, and deliver ice blocks through a contractual arrangement with the town. They were also hired by people moving from one residence to another.

Jim received neither an allowance nor any cash compensation from his father for his hours of labor. Beginning at the age of fourteen, he drove the truck regularly. He believed that one of the policemen in the town knew he was too young to drive but just ignored it because the officer also knew the circumstances which necessitated survival for the poor.

Jim sometimes skipped school to shine shoes near the local train station to make money. He recalls that once when one of his teachers saw him, she looked away and avoided eye contact as if pretending not to notice. Many years later, he interpreted that action as her simply understanding the extent of his poverty and the necessity for him to make money. With no mother, washer, or dryer, he often had to wear the same clothes for long periods. He recalled that once, one of his teachers asked him if he could come to school a little cleaner. Her question was within earshot of other students. He remembered feeling hurt, uncomfortable, and embarrassed.

He spent many long hours working on his father's truck. He did not enjoy that type of work but put forth his best effort to keep his father happy. He remembered working and then going immediately to basketball practice. One afternoon, on the day of a critical game, he helped his father carry a ton of coal (26 bushels) up several flights of stairs before the game.

Life Can Be Beautiful

He experienced many long and lonely nights wondering just how his future would evolve. His father, who had only finished seventh grade, never encouraged him or his brothers to succeed in academics or sports. His childhood was not filled with a lot of happy memories. Unrest, turmoil, inadequate food, and tattered clothing were commonplace for him. Yet, during those challenges, Jim remembered his father often times saying, "Life can be beautiful."

He always enjoyed going to school and gaining knowledge; however, he never had a favorite teacher. The schools in Aliquippa, Pennsylvania were integrated during those times, whereas many schools in the Midwest and South were not. He never had an African American teacher until he enrolled at a Historically Black College (HBCU), Lincoln University in Jefferson City, Missouri. He never would have enrolled in any college had he followed the script that his high school counselor had written for him. She enrolled him in the electrician curriculum so that he would be able to get a job when he finished high school. This action indicates that she probably believed he would not go to college due to his poverty status and perhaps his race. During that time, taking up a trade or going to a trade school was designed for those students who would not likely attend college.

He became interested in sports very early in life. He played on the sixth - grade basketball team at Jones School, which has since been demolished. Baseball and softball were also sports in which he participated. He played basketball as often as possible throughout his years in elementary and junior high school. It was unorganized play and took place wherever he and other boys could find a basketball and a place to shoot baskets. Sometimes the basketball net was a creative replica: often a bushel basket with the bottom removed. Obviously, this was not an ideal situation, but he practiced and played anyway. As a youth, two of his heroes were Jesse Owens, the Olympic track champion who won four gold medals in the 1936 Olympic Games, and Jackie Robinson, the professional baseball player who broke the color barrier in Major League Baseball.

He recalled that as a youngster, he often dreamed of seeing the world. He pictured going on journeys to "Those Faraway Places, With the Strange-Sounding Names," which he had read about many times and thought about when he heard those words in one of his favorite songs, "Far Away Places," made famous by Bing Crosby and Vera Lynn. His father's often repeated words, "Life Can Be Beautiful," resonated with him. Those dreams, experiences, and his father's words gave him hope, a sense of wonderment, and a desire to travel, and "reach for the stars."

Aliquippa High School - Academics, Athletics, Heroes, and Hopes

*A life is not important except in the impact
it has on other lives.*
Jackie Robinson

*What you are as a person is far more important
than what you are as a basketball player.*
John Wooden

*Friendships born on the field of athletic strife
are the real gold of competition. Awards become
corroded, but friends gather no dust.*
Jesse Owens

*James Frank in Flight for the Aliquippa High School Quipps
1949 State Championship Team*

When Jim went to high school, he became aware of the many advantages and opportunities for personal growth through participation in sports. For the first time, he had a coach and participated in organized sports. He played on his high school basketball team and was co-captain, with Michael "Mickey" Zernich, during his senior year. Zernich kept a long white rope in the locker room at school, and every time the team won, he tied a knot in the rope. He also carried a harmonica on the bus when they traveled to games and always entertained his teammates with music, including the school alma mater. Zernich went to the University of Pittsburgh on a basketball scholarship and later became an orthopedic surgeon. Jim and Mickey had mutual respect. They became best friends after high school and remained close confidants until Mickey passed away in 2014. He was laid to rest with that famous harmonica in his hands.

During the time Dr. Frank played basketball in high school, there were two other African Americans on the team, Richard Billingsly and Clarence "Bud" Shaw. However, the high school student population was a mixture of many ethnic groups. During those years, he developed close friendships and learned the true meaning of sportsmanship - concepts that would last and shape his lifelong philosophy. He learned the importance of teamwork, leadership, competitiveness, persistence, and grace in winning and losing.

In Aliquippa High School, the gym and auditorium were in proximity, so, while practicing basketball in the gym, he could often hear the senior class practicing to the tune of "Pomp and

Circumstance." That melody made him want to graduate from high school so that he could also march to the tune of that beautiful, riveting, graduation march song.

His high school days were filled with many memorable moments and events. During his freshman year, he decided to try out for football in addition to playing basketball. He suited up for practice, was assigned the position of linebacker, and was ready to play. During the first play, he was hit by a large, robust player, knocked to the ground, and actually "saw stars." He immediately decided that football was not his calling. However, it was the sport for his youngest brother, Willie, who also played at Aliquippa High. Albert, another brother, played baseball. The three Frank brothers were highly regarded and were extremely fortunate to be successfully engaged in sports at that time in their lives.

Despite Jim's decision not to play football, he so loved being involved in the sports arena that he asked the coach if he could be a football manager. The coach allowed him to be a manager for the football team for four years – freshman through senior years in high school. He was the first African American student to be a football manager at Aliquippa High School. During that period in history, the accomplishment was noteworthy, and that was the beginning of the many times he would earn the title, "the first." Dr. Frank thoroughly enjoyed the position of the football manager. He also looked forward to the two-week summer camps because he was assured three meals a day and comfortable, spacious sleeping quarters – all luxuries for this poor kid from Aliquippa, Pennsylvania.

Jackie Robinson – Witnessing a Hero

While in high school, one of his most memorable moments was going to Forbes Field in Pittsburgh, Pennsylvania to see Jackie Robinson play. Dr. Frank was sixteen years old when one of his older brothers, Robert, took him to the game. He had a vivid recollection of that game. The Pittsburgh Pirates played Robinson's Brooklyn Dodgers, and Brooklyn won the game.

He appreciated Robert's taking him because Jim understood Jackie Robinson's obstacles as the pioneer Black athlete to break the color barrier in professional baseball. He always admired Jackie for his courage, talent, grit, and intelligence. Dr. Frank considered Jackie Robinson his "Hero."

As a foreshadowing of his future, approximately twenty years later, after marrying and later receiving his doctorate, Dr. Frank's career took him to New York. Jackie Robinson was also living there during that time. Although he never met Jackie, Jim had been recruited and mentored by a close friend of Robinson's, Mal Goode, the history-making African American newscaster who later became Jim's very good friend. Also, over the years, he met and got to know one of Jackie's teammates, Roy Campanella, considered one of the greatest catchers in the history of the game and voted into the Major League Baseball Hall of Fame. Dr. Frank and Campanella lived in neighborhoods that were not far apart. When getting together, they reminisced about many historical moments in professional baseball.

Aliquippa High School Basketball Team.
1949 Pennsylvania State Champions

State Champions and other Electrifying Moments.

Dr. Frank vividly recalled his greatest moment at Aliquippa High School. During his senior year, the basketball team went undefeated in a 29-game hectic schedule with a record of 29-0. As the team's second-highest scorer, he was elected to the all-state team. Achieving an undefeated season was an incredible accomplishment. The whole town was exuberant. The big parade and many celebrations were full of joy and laughter. Bragging rights and happy memories remain today as part of ongoing conversations among native Aliquippians. Incidentally, the nickname for the team was the "Quips." As of this writing, that record of wins has not been broken. In conversations with family and friends, Dr. Frank flashed a wide smile when he re-lived those moments.

Also, during his senior year, students voted for the annual king and queen. Although Dr. Frank's very good friend, Michael "Mickey "Zernich, reportedly won, it was rumored that Dr. Frank had won, but those in control had altered the vote total because of his race. During the assembly, when Zernich was announced as the King, one outraged Black female student yelled, "Not Living!" She was reprimanded but allowed to return to class. That was one of many racial incidents that took place in the integrated Aliquippa High School, and of course, there were others. In S. L. Price's book, Playing Through the Whistle, he wrote: "Each fall about a dozen Black boys and girls enrolled at Aliquippa High, and when it came time for square dancing in Miss Elizabeth Carver's class, Blacks were not allowed to dance with whites. For many, that was the first time they'd feel what some dubbed "a racial" blatant prejudice."[5] Prejudice was indeed part of the Aliquippa experience.

Dr. Frank could look back on his years in Aliquippa High School with fond memories, having been an all-around athlete and scholar whose contributions to the school will always be in the annals of the school's history. He was the second-highest scorer in the state. He also played shortstop on his high school baseball team, finishing his junior year with a .400 batting average. Additionally, he played baseball with the American Legion Team. Although he excelled in baseball and basketball, he liked playing basketball best of all. His outstanding academic record and outgoing personality earned him the position of vice-president of the National Honor Society. And, in the end, he finally marched to the tune of "Pomp

---

[5] Price, Playing, 99

and Circumstance" which he had so often heard echoing, from the auditorium down the hall, as he practiced basketball in the gym.

Rounding the bases for the Aliquippa High School Quips

When Dr. Frank left high school, he looked back on years well spent: years of athletic and academic accomplishments, years of character building and goal setting, and years during which he developed lifelong friendships with his classmates and teammates. He remained close friends with two of his teammates, Dr. Michael Zernich, co-captain of the high school basketball team, and Jerry Montini, who became the principal of Aliquippa High School. Bernie Juth, another classmate, also remained one of his close friends. He always valued friendships and family, feeling there were no substitutes for them.

Melancholy High School Farewell

As he left Aliquippa High School in May 1949, he took in his memory and soul the words of his high school alma mater which he would sometimes hum and sing throughout his life. He had many fond memories of his high school days, the lifelong friendships he developed, the high school song, the colors, the sports competition, the long walk from his home to the high school, his involvement in high school organizations, and his dedicated coach, Mr. Sam Malanovich. Mr. Malanovich was a great motivator and was successful in getting the most out of his basketball players. He taught players to be unselfish and to possess a real team spirit. Those significant lessons motivated him to graduate with a desire to continue his education.

The words to his beloved high school Alma Mater follow:

"Wave Red and Black Forever Wave"

Wave, Red and Black, Forever Wave,
Unfurl aloft our fairest name,
Wave Red and Black Forever Wave,
We praise thy virtuous fame,
Fight on to conquer for our banner,
And may our spirit never die,
Wave Red and Black Forever Wave,
For Aliquippa High

The time had come for Dr. Frank to bid farewell to his beloved Aliquippa High School. The big question looming in his mind at that point was, "And Now What?" After graduation, he did not know what his next move would be. Although he was an honor student, vice president of the National Honor Society, an All-State basketball player, CO-Captain of the basketball team, a letterman in baseball, and his high school was well-known for producing good athletes, he was offered only two partial scholarships. One was from the University of Michigan and the other was from Davis /Elkins University in West Virginia. His race, no doubt, was a factor because during those days Afro American players were not heavily recruited to attend large, predominantly White institutions. He thought about moving to another state, but "where" and "how" were the questions that kept him awake at night. It would take money to do that, and he had none. However, despite the obstacles, he continued to optimistically contemplate his future. Even at that young age, he was probably theorizing what he would later often say in interviews, "My basic belief in perseverance is what helped me along the way. You aren't going to get there if you don't persevere." Then one day something happened that would change his life forever, and send him on an ever-upward trajectory.

The Unexpected Guests

One afternoon in June 1949, while Dr. Frank was sitting on his porch talking to a friend, a man named Raymond Kemp, the basketball coach at Lincoln University, a Historically Black University (HBCU) in Jefferson City, Missouri, came to his house. He wanted to talk to him about accepting a full scholarship to attend Lincoln University. Mr. Kemp had played for the Pittsburgh Steelers in 1933, one of two Blacks to play in the NFL during the first attempts to integrate teams. He had brought along with him, his good friend, Mr. Mal Goode, the first Black news reporter for a major television network, ABC, and later a United Nations correspondent. Living in Pittsburgh, Mr. Goode had read about Jim and told his good friend, Ray Kemp, he needed to go and talk to Jim Frank about playing ball for Lincoln. Ironically, Jim and those two men would later become lifelong friends.

During that visit, Dr. Frank recalled not being excited about going to a university or city about which he knew nothing. However, he did know enough to realize that an opportunity to attend college on a full scholarship was something he could not afford to turn down. He also knew that it was the only full scholarship offer he had received and that it most certainly would be better than his only other option which was working in the J and L Steel Mill. He also took note of what Mr. Mal Goode said to him: It did not matter where he went to college, it did matter what kind of person he was and what he would be doing ten years hence. In the end, it is character that matters.

Jim made a promise to Mr. Kemp that he would think about the offer and get in touch with him. It did not take long for him to reach a decision. He later contacted Mr. Kemp and accepted the full scholarship offer. He worked in the steel mill during the summer of 1949. He needed only a tiny amount of time to pack his meager belongings in preparation for the long train ride to enroll at Lincoln University. Excelling in academics and sports enabled him to move away from the steel mill town of Aliquippa and onto a new playing field.

There were some other notable Americans who came from Aliquippa and surrounding Beaver County, Pennsylvania. One non-sport notable from the area was the *Pink Panther* composer Henry Mancini. Some sports notables were Darrelle Revis, Ty Law, Tony Dorsett, Press Maravich, Pete Maravich, and Hall of Fame football coach Mike Ditka, who also graduated from Aliquippa High School. Dr. Frank and Mike Ditka were inducted into the Aliquippa Sports Hall of Fame at the same time in 1976. Ditka has a chapter titled "Aliquippa" in his autobiography.[6] In it, he speaks about his father's and grandfather's degrading work in the J & L mill and how school and sports were also his paths away from that life.

---

[6] Mike Ditka, *Ditka, An Autobiography* (Chicago, Bonus Books, Inc., 1986)

Chapter 3

Lincoln University
– A New Playing Field

*Jim Frank is our most promising freshman cager this
year, and in seasons to come, he should develop into one
of Lincoln University's finest.*
Raymond Kemp

There is no better place to learn life skills than athletics.
Cedric Dempsey

*College days swiftly pass, imbued with memories fond,
and the recollection slowly fades away.*
Taken from the Alpha Phi Alpha Fraternity Hymn

*James Frank, lower left, with other Lettermen Athletes on the steps of Stamper
Hall, Lincoln University, Missouri*

Pittsburgh, Pennsylvania is about thirty miles north of Aliquippa. He chose to take the train out of Pittsburgh. He left home early one cool morning in August 1949 with his brother, Robert, driving him and seeing him off in Pittsburgh to board the train for the long ride to Missouri. Once on the train, he intermittently felt lonely, ambivalent, sad, and fearful, but feelings of excitement, happiness, adventure, and wonderment prevailed. As the train trudged along, he was witnessing sights and sounds of parts of the United States he had only read about in books and newspapers. Little did he realize that this was the beginning of many adventures into unknown territories that his journey through life would take him. Many exciting adventures awaited him.

When the train went through East St. Louis, he woke up from a short nap, looked out the window, and thought, *where am I? Am I passing through a city, or is this my destination? Passing the* run-down part of that city, he let out a sigh of relief that he had not yet reached Jefferson City. He was still somewhat anxious about his destination. Once the train rolled into Jefferson City, he let out another sigh of relief but this time for a different reason. He was glad to have finally arrived at the place where he would begin his college career and continue playing his beloved basketball. And, having always been adventurous, he was eagerly looking forward to getting off the train and going on the campus to survey the entire environment. After all, for this poor teenager from Aliquippa who had never even been on a train, this was an uncertain but exciting time for him.

He would learn his way around the city fairly quickly because though the city seemed large to him, it indeed was not. At that time in 1949, the population of the city was about 35,000, and the student enrollment at Lincoln University was approximately three hundred. Today, student enrollment is 3,314. When he first arrived at the campus, he was in awe of its beauty, the hills, serenity, and the peaceful atmosphere that awaited him there. He gratefully smiled as he experienced a sense of contentment and purpose. Mr. Raymond Kemp, his new coach who recruited him from his front porch in Aliquippa, picked him up at the train station and showed him around, was pleased that his recruit liked the campus.

"Lincoln O Lincoln"- Exhilarating Campus Life

Lincoln University is a Historically Black 1890 land-grant, public institution. After the Civil War, the University was founded in 1866 by the officers and soldiers of the 62nd and 65th United States Colored Infantry to enable Black students to get a college education. Lincoln University is located in the capital of Missouri and has been labeled the "Black Harvard of the Midwest." After the 1954 Supreme Court decision to end school segregation and student enrollment increased tremendously, an article in Ebony Magazine identified Lincoln University as "The School that was Too Good to Die."[7] Lincoln University continues to provide quality education to a diverse student body.

Dr. Frank lived in the Pinehurst Barracks, one of the old army barracks which was still on campus during his freshman year. In

---

[7] Ebony Magazine, Article Title and Date Unknown

addition to the dormitories, the army barracks were also used for student housing. The rooms were equipped with bunk beds, and two students were assigned to a room. Ironically, his first roommate, Charlie White, was also from Pennsylvania – Coraopolis, Pennsylvania. He was an older freshman because he had been in military service.

There were not many students at Lincoln from Pennsylvania when Jim arrived. Later, as word got back to Pennsylvania about that beautiful school in the Midwest that Jim Frank had chosen to attend, more students from Pennsylvania enrolled at Lincoln, particularly from the Aliquippa/Pittsburgh area. Many of the students from Pennsylvania who attended Lincoln were athletes. The living quarters were small but sufficient. He moved into the Allen Hall dormitory during his sophomore year.

When he first saw the gymnasium, he was surprised at the size and configuration. It was smaller than his high school gym and had far fewer seats. Attendees sat on one side only; whereas, in high school, the seating was on all sides, equivalent to a gym where professional basketball games are played. However, this was not discouraging to him it was just a point of interest and amazement.

His freshman year was an introduction to a life he had never known. Growing up in Aliquippa, he attended the only high school in the town. Since all students attended the same high school, the student body was integrated although Blacks were very much in the minority and the faculty was all White. Therefore, he never had a Black teacher in high school or elementary school. He stated, "At Lincoln University, I was exposed to a different culture, one with

Black professors, Black students, and no White students or teachers. I developed a more global view and a greater appreciation for Black culture." As a result of his new enlightenment, he chose to become and remain involved in campus and community activities throughout his four years at Lincoln. Ultimately, his involvement with Lincoln University would continue and span seven decades (1949 to 2019), including many years of service on the Lincoln University Foundation Board after he retired.

He continued to excel in basketball, baseball, and academics. He once said, he would advise students to study, establish short-term and long-range goals, and get involved in the total school environment. At the end of his freshman year, his coach, Mr. Raymond Kemp, said, "Jim Frank is our most promising freshman cager this year, and in seasons to come, he should develop into one of Lincoln University's finest." Jim made 200 points on 77 field goals and 46 free throws in his first season. That equates to a 10.5-point per-game average for the season of 19 games. He was indeed a gifted basketball player and an academic scholar. In line with his modesty, he tended not to overplay either of his God-given gifts. In addition to his desire to fulfill the requirements of his four-year scholarship and to put forth his best efforts on all fronts, he looked upon extracurricular activities as a standard and exciting part of college life.

One of the most memorable and significant events of his freshman year was pledging to the Alpha Phi Alpha Fraternity. He pledged to the fraternity in the spring of 1950, his freshman year, and completed initiation in the fall of 1950. The regular procedure was to follow in that order, pledge the second semester of freshman year, and complete the progression the first semester of sophomore year. He was elected president of the Sphinx Club composed of the young men who had pledged to the fraternity. The presidency was a high-profile and coveted position.

Another significant occurrence was his enrollment in the freshman algebra class, necessary because he lacked the required number of credits in math to enroll in the regular freshman college math course. He lacked those credits because he had been advised by his high school counselor to register in the Industrial Curriculum rather than the academic College Preparatory Curriculum. One result of his enrollment in that class was he met a young lady, Juanella Mae Lloyd, who nine years later would become his sister-in-law when he married her sister, Zelma Lloyd. That wonderful set of circumstances will be shared later.

While still a sophomore, he continued to star in basketball and excelled in the classroom. He was always analytical and enjoyed the pursuit of knowledge. Again, he made the honor roll and was inducted into the National Honor Society. He knew that he could excel in both areas and made every effort to do so. He merely repeated his success in high school.

During his junior year, he became captain of the basketball team and remained in that position throughout his junior and senior years. He considered that to be a true honor and knew that the job carried many responsibilities. He also served as Director of Intramural Sports. Perhaps one of his most pivotal decisions was to enlist in the Lincoln University Army Reserve Officer Training

Corps (ROTC). By doing that, Jim committed to the United States Army to undergo military training and become a commissioned officer upon graduation from college. The commitment meant that his first step after college would be a tour of duty with the Army. Like his brother Robert before him, Jim would serve his country in the armed forces.

Head Coach, Dwight Reed, asked him to run Cross Country track during his senior year, so he decided to try. Although he never felt a strong desire to participate in track, he put forth his best effort, as usual, and in the end, he lettered in track. That accomplishment was an excellent example of his philosophy that one should strive to be the best at whatever he or she does. He knew that track was not one of his greatest strengths, so his pursuits in that field were short-lived. He was, during that year, awarded the honor of "Most Versatile Athlete." That was the highest award given to an athlete. At the time, he secretly harbored feelings that he did not deserve the honor. He later assessed his involvement and decided that he had earned and deserved that distinction.

He recalled with laughter one of the lesser occurrences during his senior year. Dr. Frank always took a full load of courses, so in his senior year, he only needed twelve credit hours. He thought it would be a hectic free year, and it was. He majored in physical education and minored in biology, so two of the courses he took in his senior year were in the biological sciences. He remembered how silly he felt running around campus catching insects for one of the class assignments. He just surmised that the assignment was all a part of the college experience. He knew the end of his college days was quickly approaching, and he would look back on those days with pride. He took pride in having put forth his best effort both on the basketball court and in the classroom. Jim had a very successful college experience and graduated from Lincoln University with honors.

A Fond and Sentimental Farewell

Now the grand terminating prize had finally arrived – time for graduation. Jim entered his final year with both joy and sadness. He knew the end of the kind of life he had known for four great years was about to end. He would miss playing the game he loved, the many close friendships he had developed, college life, and the beautiful campus, all of which now held so many fond memories for him. He would genuinely miss spending time with his last college roommate, Conrad "Connie" Carrington, from Toronto, Canada. They had become best friends. Through that friendship, he had spent three summers in Toronto with the Carrington family. He became a part of their family, and that kinship lasted a lifetime. Incidentally, Connie and his sister, Iris, are both graduates of Lincoln University, and one brother, Martin, attended Lincoln.

He considered graduation day both a culmination and a turning point. The journey would continue. Connie was also graduating, so his family came from Toronto, Canada, to attend the graduation. Because of the role they had played in Jim's life, and none of his immediate family members were in attendance, the Carrington presence was especially significant to him. He remembered long and sentimental farewells to classmates, friends, professors, and adopted family members. College graduation marked the end of a long, memorable, unique, educational, unforgettable, "cannot be duplicated" experience. God's presence was evident throughout the journey, and it was time to move on to higher ground.

Chapter 4

Higher Duty, Higher Education, Holy Matrimony, And A Return to Lincoln University

Those who say it can't be done are
usually interrupted by others doing it.
James Baldwin

Knowledge is Power.
Francis Bacon

You can always go back to where you came from
when you've done right at where you were.
James Frank

Jim Frank Playing All-Star-Championship Basketball in Korea as a Lieutenant
in the U.S. Army Corps of Engineers

The long-standing slogan of the Reserve Officer Training Corps (ROTC) was then, and still is today, "Leadership Excellence." Jim's movement into the Army was another transformative step in his iconic journey. The transitional ROTC summer training, otherwise known as summer camp, is young cadets' final basic military skills training, preparation, and indoctrination before being commissioned as officers and sent to their specific schools to train in their military specialty or branch. The camp usually takes place after a student's junior year in college. However, in his case, Jim attended after his senior year because ROTC was not offered at Lincoln University until his sophomore year, and he did not enroll until his junior year.

He went to summer camp in Colorado Springs, Colorado, at Camp Carson, now Fort Carson, and was commissioned a second lieutenant around the same time that the U.S., North Korean, and South Korean military commanders and government officials culminated their ceasefire negotiations in Korea. Since he was designated an engineer in the Engineer Corps, he proceeded to the Engineer Officer Basic Course at Fort Belvoir, Virginia. In the fall of 1953, after completing the course, he took additional training there until the end of September. He was deployed to Seoul, South Korea in March 1954. This was another "far away" place for Jim Frank. On active duty, he began what would be fourteen months in the prior war zone of South Korea, which had signed an armistice only eight months before his arrival. Little did Jim know that serving his country in the armed forces would not only provide him with life-changing leadership training and experience and a chance to see other parts of the world but would also allow him to continue to do something he loved to do, play basketball. During his time in Korea, he was selected to play on the Army Korean All-Star team and participated in the Army Far East Tournament. This was yet another excellent opportunity for him to strengthen his leadership skills and character through the teambuilding and relationship-building process of his favorite team sport.

Army Lieutenant Jim Frank at the orphanage he
helped build near Seoul, Korea

Article in hometown paper announces Lt. Frank's
request for support for the Korean orphanage.

Jim also played an active role in creating and building a children's orphanage near his duty station in Seoul. That experience was gratifying, particularly as he came to know some of the children. He called upon his hometown population, through the local Aliquippa newspaper, to help the cause of the orphans by making financial contributions.   The newspaper published a picture of him as part of an appeal to the public. It was a very successful project and marked the end of his two-year commitment to the Army. Without question, Jim believed that by serving in the United States Army, he was answering the call to a higher duty. He was proud to be a military Veteran.

At the end of his tour, Jim could have easily continued in the service and even sought a career in the military, but he determined, at that time, that he wanted to pursue higher education. He had his sights set on a college that he held in high esteem for quite some time - Springfield College in Springfield, Massachusetts. One of his closest friends from college, Don Hudson, who was also in the military in Korea, talked about getting a master's degree there as well. So, after completing his military service in 1955, Jim Frank enrolled at Springfield College to seek his master's degree in physical education.

A statue of James Naismith who invented basketball
at Springfield College in Massachusetts

Higher Education and the Journey Back to Lincoln University

Springfield College and the city of Springfield would play a significant role in Jim's life. He had read a lot about the college and its mission to develop spirit, mind, and body. He not only obtained his master's degree there, but he began forging lifelong friendships during that time. Tommy and Betty Thomas, Jesse, and Lucile Parks, Reggie and Rachel Stockton, and Jean and Cliff Flint were some of the early relationships. Basketball was born at Springfield College and is the home of the Naismith Memorial Hall of Fame and Museum in honor of James Naismith who invented basketball. Naismith invented the game of basketball in 1891 while a graduate student and instructor at Springfield College. It is another beautiful irony of Dr. Frank's journey that he would pursue his higher education at the home of basketball's origin and his name is on the Springfield College "List of Notable Alumni," along with Naismith.

He would return to that college several years after earning his master's to take the pursuit of education even higher and earn his doctorate. In the ensuing years, he went back again, this time to serve on the Board of Trustees.

Coach Frank in the Lincoln University Faculty Yearbook 1956-1957

In 1956, after completing his master's, Jim's alma mater, Lincoln University, opened its doors of opportunity to him once again. Athletics Director, Dwight Reed, his former college basketball coach, asked him to return to Lincoln that year as an assistant professor and assistant basketball coach. Dr. Frank was grateful for the opportunity to return to his alma mater in those positions.

When he went back to Lincoln, this time as an employee, he again lived in the Allen Hall Dormitory. Dr. Oliver Cox, a lawyer, sociologist, nationally known author, and sociology professor at Lincoln, lived across the hall from him. Dean of Students, Dr. Charles Hoard, had suggested to Dr. Frank that he live in the dormitory and serve as a counselor and advisor. He did not have to pay rent and never had any trouble with student behavior. After about one year, the young Professor Frank moved from the dormitory to an upstairs apartment in the home of a Jefferson City resident. He never dreamed that he would one day return to his Alma Mater as a professor and coach.

The Sound of Wedding Bells

During his first year in the new position, he met a young lady who was a senior in college. When he saw her on campus, he commented to one of his former classmates, Johnnie Palmer, who was then working in the business office at Lincoln University, that the young lady looked very familiar. Johnnie told him that she looked familiar because she and her sister resembled each other and reminded him that he had been in a freshman algebra class with her sister, Juanella Lloyd. He found the story so amusing that he repeated the episode to the young lady who looked familiar – Zelma Lloyd. The repeating of the story took place on campus at an AKA and Alpha dance he chaperoned. It was a brief and enjoyable casual conversation.

After that interaction, at least a month passed before they saw each other again – this time at an AKA and Alpha dinner in the University cafeteria. They communicated recognition through glances and smiles from across the room. After dinner and a brief exchange, he said he was going to walk with her to the dormitory. He and the young lady became friends, and shortly thereafter began dating. It was neither unprofessional nor unacceptable for a professor and student to date, particularly since they were only a few years apart in age. The following year, in 1957, that young lady graduated from Lincoln University, worked there during the summer, then went back to her hometown, Kansas City, Missouri. They continued their relationship, and in July 1958, she became Zelma (Lloyd) Frank.

They were married in Springfield, Massachusetts in July during the time Jim was working on his doctorate at Springfield College. They were married by Rev. Charles Cobb in the St. John's Congregational Church parsonage. They attended that church while living in Springfield. Rev. Cobb was a nationally known civil rights activist, the first executive director of the United Church of Christ's Commission for Racial Justice, and the first African American mayoral candidate in Springfield (1965). Only a few close friends and a couple of relatives were invited to the ceremony. Those in attendance were Don and Florence Hudson, Syd and Norah Hall, Connie Carrington and his friend, Franklin Lloyd and his wife Jean. Jim and Zelma were married for 60 years. Lincoln alumni often joke that long-lasting marriage seems to be the norm for people who meet at Lincoln University. After summer school, the couple returned to Lincoln University as Mr. and Mrs. Frank.

Head Basketball Coach Frank with some of his starters circa 1958

During those most wonderful developments, Jim was promoted from assistant professor and assistant basketball coach to associate professor and head basketball coach. It was evident that he shared with his players, mutual respect, and love for the game. In his new position leading the basketball team, Coach Frank quickly achieved winning seasons leading the team to an invitation to participate in the NCAA Championship tournament. He took the team to four regional NCAA Division II Championship Tournaments within only a few years of the NCAA, the organization that he would one day lead, even allowing HBCUs to participate in the tournaments. Before 1958, HBCU's had not been invited to participate in Division II NCAA Championship Tournaments, so Black colleges staged their own tournaments. This timing in history could not have been more divinely ordered. Coach Frank's accomplishments and their historical timing were placing him on the path to becoming an American icon.

There were many home and away basketball games. After 1958, the Athletics Director, Dwight Reed, initiated a trip in December. Although Dr. Frank enjoyed traveling with the team, there was one trip that he did not look forward to taking. That was the trip north to Bemidji State University in Bemidji, Minnesota, and South Dakota State in Huron, South Dakota during the Christmas holidays. That was the coldest time of year to be traveling to some of the coldest parts of the country. The team traveled by bus, and Mrs. Frank also went on these trips. Her memories include chilling cold weather, being the only female on board, talking to one of the bus drivers late at night to keep him awake while everyone else was asleep, and not being hungry enough to eat three full meals a day every day as scheduled. However, the basketball players expected and had no trouble consuming three meals a day plus snacks.

In 1959, the number of Black teachers in the Jefferson City, Missouri public school system was minuscule because of discriminatory hiring practices. During that period, there were two African American teachers in the entire school system. Mrs. Frank, having received her bachelor's degree in elementary education, decided to teach in her hometown, Kansas City, Missouri. However, her first teaching assignment was in Kansas City, Kansas, for one year (1957-1958). She left the Kansas system due to her upcoming marriage. At that time, a person could not be married and teach in the Kansas City, Kansas Public School System. So, during the two years after marriage, she taught in the Kansas City, Missouri Public School System (1958-1960). The Franks lived in different cities for those two years and only saw each other on weekends except when Dr. Frank had to travel somewhere with the basketball team. Getting together entailed Dr. Frank driving to Kansas City, or Mrs. Frank driving to Jefferson City.

The Birth of a Son

Mrs. Frank joined her husband in Jefferson City in 1960. Shortly after Mrs. Frank moved to Jefferson City, they purchased a side-by-side duplex. They rented out one side to Mary Louise Savage, a long-time English professor at Lincoln University, who had a young son named Gregory. Mrs. Savage was a highly regarded professor who had worked at Lincoln University when both Jim and Zelma were students there. She was a great tenant, neighbor, and friend.

In 1961, their first son, Trent Terence Frank, was born. The circumstances of his birth warrant notation here. Despite the Mid-Missouri February weather, Mrs. Frank, in her ninth month of pregnancy, attended her husband's basketball game. It was a very cold winter night, and the snow was falling heavily. During the game, she became very uncomfortable and had to leave the gymnasium. Jim had one of their close friends, Alonzo "Candy" Brown, drive her to the hospital, and it became evident that she was to deliver soon. Coach Frank was called, and he had to turn coaching duties over to his good friend and colleague, Don Hudson, and leave the game to go to the hospital and be with his wife. The action went on in the gym while a different kind of action was taking place at the hospital. Jim and Zelma, as well as Lincoln University, were victorious that night.

Dr. Frank thoroughly enjoyed working at Lincoln University. Again, placing great value on friendships, Dr. Frank enjoyed golfing on weekends and socializing with two of his closest friends and their families, Don Hudson and Alonzo "Candy" Brown who was also teaching at Lincoln. However, it was his mission in the area of athletics and education that gave him the greatest rewards. At one point, he made the following statement, "I enjoyed my role as a teacher and coach tremendously. It offered me an opportunity to affect the lives of students and colleagues in a very positive way." Dr. Frank continued to work at Lincoln until 1963 when he applied for and was granted sabbatical leave to complete his doctorate at Springfield College.

Chapter 5

Back East - New Horizons

*Trust in the Lord with all thine heart and lean not unto
thine own understanding; in all thy ways acknowledge
Him, and He shall direct thy paths.*
Proverbs 3:6

*Help others, share your knowledge,
counsel, guide, and teach.*
James Frank

*Jim, Zelma, Trent, and newborn Troy at Bernard and Shelly Gutin's home in
White Plains, New York*

Professor Frank never really wholly left Springfield or Springfield College after completing his master's degree. In addition to being the location of his marriage to Zelma, it remained in his heart, mind, and doctoral plans. In 1963, professor Frank was awarded a sabbatical leave to go back to Springfield College and complete the course requirements for his Doctor of Physical Education Degree (D.P.E.). This degree merged his two passions for higher education and athletics.

Welcome sign on Campus at Springfield College

He had completed some course requirements during one summer there at Springfield and also while attending the University of Kansas (KU) during one summer session. Mrs. Frank also attended KU that same summer; they were enrolled in one class together and sat side by side. That was an interesting, fun, and different experience, and yes, sometimes challenging as Professor

Frank questioned Mrs. Frank's note-taking acumen. He later laughingly denied having ever done that.

Dr. Frank was grateful for the opportunity afforded him by Lincoln to complete his doctoral studies. While completing his doctorate, he worked as a student assistant and taught courses. Meanwhile, Mrs. Frank taught first grade at DeBerry Elementary School in Springfield. Their combined salaries made the economic side of their lives very pleasurable. They were blessed to find suitable childcare facilities for their young son, Trent. Life in Springfield was an enjoyable experience, even though that winter was frigid. In addition to earlier friendships forged in Springfield, they developed many more lifelong friendships. Eleanor Roosevelt said, "Many people will walk in and out of your life, but only true friends will leave footprints in your heart." The Franks had an exceptional group of true friends with whom they socialized on weekends. Also, during the weekends, Dr. Frank and some of his friends engaged in one of his favorite sports, golf.

Weekdays, out of necessity, were pretty much regimented. At home in the evenings after work, Dr. Frank was usually engrossed in spending time with his son, studying, researching, and writing his dissertation. Mrs. Frank was immersed in cooking, childcare, and typing the dissertation. The evenings were quiet and peaceful. Recalling that period brings to mind many fond memories of working, conversing, goal setting, and planning for the future while living in their comfortable apartment. It was a good life, and the writer is thankful for the memories.

In 1962, Dr. Frank received his doctorate from Springfield College. Dr. Martin Luther King, Jr. was the keynote speaker at the graduation. His speech was masterful. The Franks were grateful for the opportunity to meet and speak with him after the ceremony. Those were some special moments.

The newly christened Dr. Frank had planned to return to Lincoln University for at least one year, as required under the guidelines for accepting a sabbatical leave. However, Dr. Dawson, president of Lincoln at that time, felt that Jim's doctorate degree overqualified him for college coaching, so he released him from the obligation to return. Dr. Frank did not agree with the president's decision. Additionally, he was disappointed because he had planned to fulfill his obligation to return and was looking forward to coaching basketball at Lincoln once again. Nevertheless, he began exploring other avenues for the next step in his journey. Ironically, many years later, Dr. Frank would return to Lincoln as president, and occupy the same residence in which Dr. Dawson had resided.

Unplanned Move to New York

During his subsequent job search, Dr. Frank found opportunities for himself and his wife in New York where they would both be teaching in the Greenburgh, District 8 Public School System. After receiving his doctorate in 1964, he moved his family to White Plains in Westchester County. They lived in the town of Greenburgh.

Not having ever taught in public schools, Dr. Frank thought teaching at the high school level would be an exciting experience and would add to his depth of knowledge in education. Having been a college professor, accustomed to lecturing to young adults, he found his job responsibilities from college to high school very different from what he had been accustomed to performing. He worked at Woodlands High School in Hartsdale, N.Y. Hall duty, bus duty, cafeteria monitoring, and after-school detention hall were job requirements he had never experienced. He found them somewhat frustrating and not in line with his overall goals. Dr. Frank had always looked forward to going to work in the past, but that changed when he started teaching in high school. He would jokingly wish for "snow days," which meant school would be closed due to hazardous or inclement weather conditions.

Nevertheless, as he had always done, Dr. Frank sought to serve and make things better for others in any way he could, particularly when it came to education. Although teaching in high school was not his calling, he did have an enduring desire to see improvement in the education of children in the district. He reflected on the formative impact of his own high school experiences. Dr. Frank became involved in community activities and provided his leadership wherever he felt there was a need. He attended a Baptist church in the community where the Pastor's daughter was a student in Mrs. Frank's fifth-grade class.

One such involvement led to Dr. Frank's initiating and becoming president of a community organization called Concerned Citizens, which was developed to help improve and implement guidelines for teacher effectiveness and student achievement. The group was also a "think tank" which monitored what was going on in the school district in all areas of the educational environment. The organization met monthly at his house, and members of the group included parents, teachers, and school secretaries. Mrs. Frank attended all of the meetings and also served as a hostess. She was still teaching in the District 8 School System at that time. Her position increased her knowledge about all of the agenda items.

The meetings, though dealing with serious issues, were usually upbeat. The Franks looked forward to the meetings, which provided an occasion to socialize while simultaneously taking care of business. The group appreciated Dr. Frank's leadership and guidance. After forming the group and serving as President, he became more aware of the issues and was inspired to run for the Greenburgh School District 8 Board of Education. He ran and won.

He served on the board of education for the Greenburgh District 8 Public School System in Westchester County. The position was interesting and challenging due to the nature of the decisions that had to be made. However, he felt that his presence on the board was necessary, and his experience in educational leadership served him well. He enjoyed serving on the board of education. The Greenburgh School District was one of the most diverse in the country. The district was well-known and people studied because of the wide range of differences in race, ethnicity, income, and abilities.

Mrs. Frank found her teaching position to be one of the most interesting assignments she had held up to that point, and working in the same district where her husband was on the board of education did not create any problems or conflicts of interest. Their oldest son, Trent, started his public school education in kindergarten in that school District and attended classes there through sixth grade. Greenburg 8 will always hold special memories for the Frank family.

Before his school board service, Dr. Frank had worked at the High School level for one year. Having decided that teaching in high school was not what he wanted to do, he sought other employment opportunities even as he worked in the local education community. He felt a strong desire to return to work in higher education. His wife agreed with his assessment and goals because she knew that teaching in high school was not in his comfort zone. Together, they were in consultation in planning the next move.

They always felt there was no substitute for teamwork and talking through situations, both big and small. They valued the opinions, insights, and input from one another and attempted to listen, not just hear. They set aside Friday nights, although not the only nights for sharing thoughts, for what were their "Listening and Time-Sharing Sessions," which encompassed an extensive range of topics and emotions. Music and fresh flowers were always a part of the backdrop. The Franks made many decisions during those sessions.

Hunter College, City University of New York

HUNTER COLLEGE
WE ARE OF DIFFERENT OPINION
AT DIFFERENT HOURS BUT W
ALWAYS MAY BE SAID TO BE A
HE T ON THE SIDE OF TRU

*Façade of Hunter College of the City University
of New York with the school philosophy*

Dr. Frank applied for a teaching position at Herbert H. Lehman College, the City University of New York, in the Bronx, later renamed Hunter College of the City University of New York. He was given the option of teaching in the Bronx or at the campus on Park Avenue in Manhattan. He chose the Bronx because it was closer to his home in Greensburg, his starting point for the daily driving commute of fifty miles roundtrip. His employment at Herbert H. Lehman College marked his return to higher education.

During his tenure as a professor at Lehman College, he served as the assistant to the dean of summer school and coordinated the NCAA National Youth Sports Program. For several years, he was head track and golf coach, and coordinator of graduate studies in physical education. Dr. Frank also supervised student teachers and directed the summer tutorial program and the physical education majors program. He worked at the College from 1964 to 1970.

Their life in New York during the sixties was fulfilling both professionally and socially. However, it was a tumultuous time in American history that included the war in Vietnam, the passing of the Voting Rights Act, and the Fair Housing Act, the landing on the Moon, and of course, the Civil Rights Movement. The assassinations of John F. Kennedy, Malcolm X, Medgar Evers, Martin Luther King, and others gripped the nation during those years. Each of the losses touched the Franks deeply. Malcolm X was murdered right there in their beloved New York City, and they were especially moved in 1968 when, at the age of thirty-nine, King was assassinated in Memphis, Tennessee. Even as the entire nation mourned, his death affected them very deeply because of their brief, but personal and moving encounter with Dr. King at Jim's commencement in Springfield. They experienced a very profound sense of sadness.

Not as impactful to the entire nation, but certainly striking close to home was what happened on Tuesday, November 9, 1968. There was a major blackout across the Eastern United States affecting more than 30 million people, many of whom were without electricity for more than 12 hours. Dr. Frank was at home and worried about Mrs. Frank as she fought darkness while driving home from a class she was taking at a nearby university. With no cell phones at that time, those hours of non-communication were torturous for them.

Birth of a Son and Birth of a College

Two exciting events affected Dr. Frank in 1970. After nine months of anticipation, Jim and Zelma Frank enthusiastically welcomed their second son, Troy, on a cold, snowy night in December. When it was time for Mrs. Frank to go to the hospital that night, they called upon Nina Hepburn, a former student of hers and the teenage daughter of their good friends and neighbors Mildred and Dave Hepburn, to come to their house to watch Trent. Two days later, they brought home their precious New York-born son, Troy, almost ten years after the birth of their first son.

Medgar Evers College of the City University of New York

Additionally, that year, Dr. Frank was invited to seek employment at a college that was just beginning to take form. Through some of his colleagues, his name was submitted to help in the formation of that institution, Medgar Evers College. After his interview with then-President, Dr. Richard Trent, he was offered the position of dean of students. In accepting that position, he became the first dean of students at Medgar Evers College. He left Herbert H. Lehman College to join the educators who had been chosen to establish the new college. He was very instrumental in that effort. His interest in making education possible and affordable for students in the Brooklyn community, his experience, insight, energy, philosophy, and leadership skills made him an invaluable team member.

Medgar Evers College is a part of the City University of New York system and was the newest of the four-year colleges which make up the system. The college, located in the Bedford-Stuyvesant area of Brooklyn, New York, was sanctioned by the Board of Higher Education on November 17, 1969. Student enrollment began during the fall of 1969. The college was officially established in 1970.

Dr. Frank wanted to go to Medgar Evers College because he understood and believed in the mission and the need to establish an HBCU in Brooklyn, New York. He also wanted to get a full-time position in administration. The salary increase was also a consideration.

Medgar Evers College was created at a crucial time. During that period, a struggling predominantly Black community dealt with issues that usually had to be addressed in such communities:

poverty, crime, drug use, and the increase in single-family households. A college was needed as a means to help stem the tide of a downward trend.

The founding of a college was engaging and challenging. Early on, Mrs. Evers had to give her permission to name the college after her husband, so Dr. Frank and some of his colleagues had to meet with her. That entire process of naming the college was noteworthy. As one of the ground-floor organizers, the experience was unlike any of Dr. Frank's previous experiences. It required many long grueling hours on the job and the maximum use of his mental and creative assets. However, he remembers that whole process as one of his most exciting and challenging seasons in academia.

After having been at the college for a year, he was asked to assume the role of vice president. When he accepted that position, he became the first Vice President of Medgar Evers College. In addition to the academic side of the job, he recalls that he often had to serve as a negotiator/mediator to keep everyone on track and focused on the goals as plans for laying the foundation of a new college were emerging. The position was exciting and challenging. One of the greatest satisfactions was knowing that the new institution of higher education would make it possible for so many young, underprivileged Black youth to obtain a college education.

Over the years since that time, the college has faced many challenges, some that even threatened its existence. As of this writing, the student enrollment at Medgar Evers College is 7,156. It is a thriving university that continues to serve the needs of students who may not otherwise have the opportunity to fulfill the desire to achieve a college degree. The Medgar Evers College Motto is "We Create Success, One Student at a Time." As an added tidbit on Medgar Evers College, Iyanla Vanzant, author, lawyer, and music-lover, who currently has a show on the Oprah Winfrey Network (OWN), is a Medgar Evers College graduate. She has a fascinating story about how and why she went to Medgar Evers College.

Dr. Frank could not have anticipated what excellent chapter would come next in his journey, but he appreciated having the opportunity to be one of the individuals chosen to develop a new college. He often recalled that experience as one of the most significant in his career.

Chapter 6

Momentous Return to Lincoln University as President

*I assume this position with full knowledge
of the trials and triumphs through which I must
pass in the coming years.*
James Frank

*This opportunity was the highlight of my career because it
allowed me the opportunity to impact the lives of so many
people while giving back to an institution that has given
so much to me. The opportunity to provide leadership to
the institution that you attended is rare.*
James Frank

*Front Cover of Lincoln University National Alumni Magazine when
Dr. James Frank was appointed president in 1973. At that time, the publication
was entitled "The Harambee."*

While deeply involved in the strategic planning for developing Medgar Evers, Dr. Frank received a phone call from a very good friend, a former college classmate, and pioneering IBM executive, Earl Wilson. He informed Dr. Frank that there was a vacancy at their alma mater, Lincoln University, and the board of curators was looking for someone to fill the position of president. He encouraged Jim to apply. Jim was not at all enthusiastic about the idea of applying for the job because he was enjoying his work and liked living in New York. In addition, his wife enjoyed teaching in an elementary school and living in New York. Trent was in middle school, and leaving his friends would not be pleasant for him.

Another reason Dr. Frank was slightly ambivalent about applying was that he had applied for the position when it was vacant five years earlier but had not been chosen. Later, one of the Search Committee members told him in confidence that he had not been offered the job because some committee members thought he was too young and lacked the experience necessary to fill that position. However, after giving it further thought and having been asked by many others to apply, he reluctantly decided to go forward. So, in 1973, Dr. Frank applied for the job of president at Lincoln University, his beloved alma mater.

Even more so than before, the rich history of this institution of higher learning loomed large within the context of his possible return to become an indelible part of that history. The history of Lincoln University has been recorded as follows:

"Lincoln University was founded as Lincoln Institute in 1866 by the men of the 62nd and 65th Colored Infantry at the end of the Civil War to give freed slaves an opportunity to get a college education. The soldiers made a monthly salary of $13.00, but they sacrificed and raised nearly $6,000.00 by pooling their money. A White abolitionist, Lt. Richard Foster, helped the soldiers get the school started. He took money to Jefferson City, Missouri, and met with the legislators. He later became the school's first principal. He also taught classes. Being knowledgeable about the school's history, W. E. B. Dubois once described the school as having the 'most romantic beginning of all the historically black colleges and universities.' It has been recorded that finding a place to hold classes was a challenge, so the soldiers were forced to meet in an old, poorly maintained small building, perhaps best described as a shack. During the thirties and forties, reportedly, the entire faculty had Doctorate Degrees, and thus, the school was often referred to as the "Black Harvard of the Midwest'."[8]

---

[8] Source: Multiple public sources, Lincoln Archives, and Lincoln University Atlanta Alumni Chapter Founder's Day Program. 2011.

Lincoln University after the turn of the century

Despite its humble beginnings, Lincoln University became nationally known and respected as a superior university whose graduates were highly sought after, particularly in Missouri. When the writer applied for a job in Kansas City in 1957 after graduating from Lincoln University, the superintendent of schools reiterated that fact. In 2016, Lincoln University celebrated its sesquicentennial anniversary.

That is the brief history of Lincoln University. Although it has been recorded in different versions, the writer has found that the core facts in the history of Lincoln always remain consistent. Lincoln

University is the only institution of higher education in the United States founded by veterans of the Civil War.

Lincoln University is a United States Land Grant University accredited by The National Council for Accreditation of Teacher Education (NCATE). The U.S. Congress instituted The Morrill Act of 1862 (also *known as the "Land Grant Act"*) which allotted money to various states to provide funding for schools that would have curriculums specializing in agriculture and the mechanical arts. Lincoln University has the unique distinction of being one of only twenty HBCU Land Grant institutions in the nation and only one of two Land Grant institutions in the state of Missouri. The University of Missouri is the other Land Grant institution. Lincoln University has undergone a major transformation in the years since its early history. After the 1954 Supreme Court Decision to desegregate schools, while Mrs. Frank was still a student there, the student population became integrated, and today there are more White students and faculty than African Americans. Lincoln and West Virginia State are the only two HBCU schools where integration worked in reverse. Lincoln was featured in an Ebony magazine article titled, "The School That Was Too Good to Die."

Shortly after submitting his application, Dr. Frank was contacted and invited for an interview. Dr. Frank and his wife flew to St. Louis where the interview took place. The board member responsible for making hotel arrangements had booked a horrible, dirty, unsafe hotel. Dr. Frank knew that even one night in that hotel would be one night too many, so he immediately picked up the phone and called Earl Wilson, a resident of St. Louis, who made arrangements for accommodations at another hotel. Dr. Frank later learned that the board member who booked the room had done it to discourage him because he preferred a friend who wanted to be president. Dr. Frank was able to laugh about it later, but it was not funny at the time. The interview took place the next day.

He did not remember anything unusual about the interview. The questions were similar to those he had answered in other job interviews. It was not a long interview, but it was in-depth. There were nine members on the Board of Curators, and it seemed that each member had at least one question. He felt relaxed and confident throughout the entire process. At the conclusion, they thanked him for his interest in Lincoln University and spoke the familiar words heard by so many people after a job interview; "You will hear from us."

About two weeks later, he received a phone call inviting him back to St. Louis, Missouri, for a second interview. The call came from the chairman of the search committee. That second interview was held in a hotel in the city. The second interview did not vary considerably from the first, except that it was perhaps a little more in-depth, and the questions were more specific. Again, he felt confident that he had answered the questions well and had conducted himself in a "presidential" manner. After that interview, the second waiting period began.

He traveled back to New York and continued his important work at Medgar Evers College, knowing that the phone would ring, to forming him about the decision any day. Although he felt good about his performance during the interviews, he knew that the decision was unpredictable. It should be noted that early on, he had informed Dr. Richard Trent, President of Medgar Evers College, that he had applied for the position at Lincoln University. During that period, he had many thoughts, both pro and con, about moving back to Missouri and accepting the job if it were offered. He and his wife had long discussions about many of the "what ifs" often involved when making significant decisions.

1973 newspaper article announcing Dr. James Frank as the president of Lincoln University. The article incorrectly names him as the 13th President instead of the 14th President

About one week after the second interview, he received the call informing him that he had been chosen to become the 14th President of his Alma Mater, Lincoln University in Jefferson City, Missouri. Dr. Frank accepted the position. Although he is listed as the 14th president, he is not the 14th person to hold that position. According to Mark Schleer, Lincoln University archivist,[9] and recorded

---

[9] Phone conversations between 2019-2020

history, two of the presidents who preceded him served two non-consecutive terms, each time filling a presidential term vacancy. So, Dr. Frank was the 12th person to serve, but he was filling the 14th Presidential Term Vacancy. There were 14 presidential term vacancies filled by only 12 persons.

For additional clarification, it should be noted that the first five men who headed the University served under the title of principal, one of whom served twice. Dr. Frank was the 17th person to head the University. At the time of Dr. Frank's appointment, the numbers were as follows:

The total number of persons who had served as either principal or president was 17. The total number of principal or president term vacancies had been 20. In 1880, the sixth leader of the University, Inman E. Page, became the first person to serve under the title of president. The Lincoln University library bears his name.

Another Season Begins

Upon accepting the position, Dr. Frank was immersed in feelings of joy coupled with surges of uncertainties and wonderment. These are just some of the emotions that often accompany "New Beginnings." Leaving the familiar is sometimes difficult and fraught with a kind of loneliness. Additionally, the unknown is often suspenseful. But overall, he was acting as if he was thinking, "Count your blessings, leave any residue of uncertainty behind, and move forward quickly and with confidence."

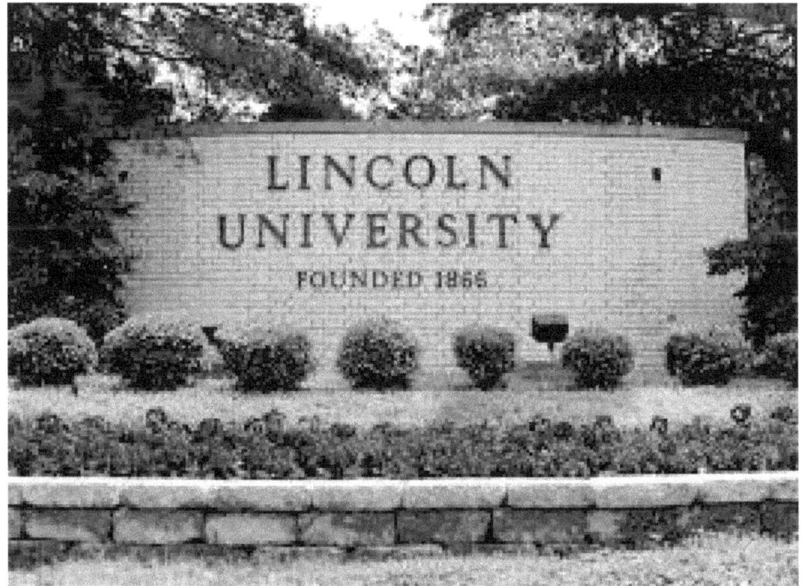

Sign at the entrance to the Lincoln University campus

In the fall of 1972, after the announcement was made public, Dr. Frank and his family were invited to the University to be introduced to faculty, staff, and students. At that time, the Frank's two sons were aged twelve and two. As the family stepped on stage in the large auditorium in Young Hall to be introduced, the loud and continuous clapping was overwhelming! Dr. Frank's wife and oldest son recall being deeply moved! That was an incredible moment - one to cherish forever.

*The historic home of Lincoln University presidents near
the campus in Jefferson City, Missouri*

The Franks were shown the house they would occupy. Built by students in the industrial arts department, the first home for Lincoln University Presidents was located on the campus. It was later torn down to build Founder's Hall. The home the Franks would occupy was also owned by the University and was a large, stone, old, impressive residence. It was the official home of the president. Only one other Presidential family had previously occupied the residence, often referred to as a mansion. That president was Dr. Dawson. In 1981, Dr. Frank's wife wrote a book on the history of the house. The book is titled, *A History of the House for Lincoln University Presidents.* The publication revealed many fascinating and little-known facts about the house. Two days after the visit, Frank and his family flew back to New York to begin the arduous task, both physical and mental, of moving from White Plains, New York, to Jefferson City, Missouri.

Dr. Frank left Medgar Evers with best wishes from his soon-to-be former boss, Dr. Richard Trent, who was president of Medgar Evers College at that time. When he got into his car and left the Brooklyn, New York campus for the last time, he certainly felt a sense of disconnect, not having stayed to see the completion of the college. He also felt a tinge of sadness coupled with a sense of gratefulness for having been able to have made significant contributions for the good of students, many of whom were destined to become future leaders. He experienced a mixture of feelings. Interestingly enough, Dr. Frank never returned to the Medgar Evers campus after the day he left in 1973. The journey of life does not always allow for repeat performances or a u-turn to travel back down a road once traveled.

After packing up everything and loading the car, he remembered just sitting in his car in front of the house they had built in the beautiful subdivision of White Plains, New York where he and his family had lived for the past ten years. His wife and two sons, Trent, and Troy were also in the vehicle, a 1969 dark green Oldsmobile. A neighbor of ten years, Dave Hepburn, journalist and vice president with WNEW-TV, who lived across the street, had already said his goodbyes and wondered why the Franks were just sitting there. He went to inquire and bid farewell again. Dr. Frank told him that they were lingering because his wife, in a sentimental mood, was reminiscing, and wanted to just stay a while longer.

Probably those were the feelings that Jim was also experiencing, but just not admitting. Mr. Hepburn smiled and said simply, "Just consider this move as the closing of one chapter and the opening of another." Those words resonated profoundly and were very prophetic because the stage was set for a glorious continuation of the opening and closing of chapters yet to come in Dr. Frank's life. After a few more long pauses, reflections, parting words, and sentiments, the Franks slowly pulled away from the curb to start the long automobile trip from White Plains, New York to Jefferson City, Missouri.

They drove as far as Jim's hometown of Aliquippa, Pennsylvania, and stayed overnight in neighboring Sewickley, Pennsylvania where his brother Albert lived. Although he had returned home quite frequently over the years for visits and family reunions, spending the night there on this trip, he reflected on how much things had changed for him since leaving Pennsylvania almost twenty-four years earlier as James Frank, a high school graduate heading to Lincoln University on a basketball scholarship. The next day he continued his journey to Missouri, this time as Dr. James Frank, president of Lincoln University.

After arriving in Jefferson City, the Franks stayed at the Holiday Inn for a short time while the University maintenance crew continued to prepare the president's house for occupancy. One night, while having dinner in the restaurant located on the top floor, they looked out the window. The view of the city paled in comparison to the bright lights, tall buildings, and busy highways that they were accustomed to seeing from top-floor restaurants in

New York. They looked at each other and almost stated in unison, "this is going to be different!" It was indeed a time of transition. They stayed at the hotel for approximately one week.

Drs. James and Zelma Frank in front of Lincoln University president's residence with sons Trent (left) and Troy (Right)

Moving In

Finally, the day came to move from the hotel into the president's residence. The hustle and bustle of unpacking was lessened because the house was furnished, so it was just unpacking personal belongings. The house is recorded in history as the Hugh Stephens House because he was the wealthy man who had the house built. The home was designed by the same architectural firm that designed the State Capitol in Jefferson City. Lincoln University currently owns the house. The home is presently listed in Historical Tours, Jefferson City, Missouri, a publication by the Jefferson City Convention and Visitors Bureau. The historical residence seemed very large to Dr. Frank's two-year-old son, Troy, who kept peeping around different corners of the house and asking, "Will I see a ghost?"

On the other hand, Trent, who was ten years older than Troy, just seemed to take everything in stride. However, in revisiting the past and recapping his thoughts at that time, he recently recalled that he had never wanted to leave New York. He had good friends, familiar and comfortable surroundings, sports, and extracurricular activities, everything he thought made for a perfect life. At the same time, he was mature enough to theorize that the move was good because it probably would result in an even better life. After all, Dr. Frank was acquiring a bigger job and looking forward to it with great anticipation. He trusted that his parents had made a thoughtful and wise decision which gave him the comfort level he needed to make peace with his conflicting emotions. He had recently shared those feelings with his parents.

Family Portrait Christmas Card with sons,
Trent (center) and Troy (Right)

The day was filled with excitement and ongoing activity as many University personnel came by the house to introduce themselves and help. Even though the house was in excellent move-in condition, remodeling details were left to the Franks' discretion. The Franks got busy doing what was necessary to maintain the elegance of this beautiful, old, huge stone mansion. In Mrs. Frank's book, she described the many renovations that had taken place at the president's house and which president was in occupancy during that particular period.

The decorating was left up to Mrs. Frank who, at that time, was not employed outside of the home. She worked with an interior decorator from the Milo Walz Furniture store. For many years, the main store had been in Jefferson City and was known for its high-quality furniture, efficient customer services, and interior decorating consultation. The Franks made many changes and additions, but no structural changes, all of which Mrs. Frank described in her book. It should be noted here that living in the president's residence was a most enjoyable experience for Dr. Frank and his family. Additionally, the University paid for a full-time housekeeper, Mrs. Helen Holmes. She was a thoughtful, kind, dependable, and professional person who became a close friend and surrogate grandmother to the Frank children. Not enough kind words can be printed about Mrs. Holmes.

The Franks and Mrs. Holmes remained friends even after the Franks left Lincoln University - in fact, until her death. Her husband, Mr. George Holmes, was also a friend of the Franks who regarded him highly. The University was also willing to hire a full-time chef for the Franks, but Dr. Frank declined the offer, saying that he preferred his wife's cooking. His wife laughingly looks back on that decision and laments that if she had allowed herself to languish in the "field of regrets," she would still be regretting that she agreed with that decision. Ironically, Mrs. Holmes ended up fulfilling much of that role by sometimes partnering In the kitchen with Mrs. Frank and becoming the de facto part-time chef of the household and Troy's frequent babysitter which went above and beyond her professional duties as a Lincoln University employee.

For this relationship, the Frank family will remain forever grateful to Mrs. Holmes and her family.

The University also hired an official hostess for the presidential family. The hostess was someone already employed at the university in an additional capacity. The first hostess was Ms. Velma Thomas, a very knowledgeable, kind, and gentle home economics professor. Mrs. Frank learned a lot from her about all aspects of hosting. Mrs. Frank had never before had to serve in that capacity so often.

Upon the death of Ms. Thomas, Ms. Sheila Logan was assigned to replace her. Ms. Logan was employed in the University Center. She was also very knowledgeable about the job. She was cheerful and creative. Ms. Logan enjoyed performing her duties and making guests feel welcome. She and the Frank family shared mutual love and respect and developed a lifelong friendship.

Mr. President

So now began the season in Dr. Frank's life when he was president of Lincoln University. He was appointed president on July 1, 1973. This phase of his life could compose a separate book as could other seasons such as being SWAC Commissioner. When Dr. Frank was named president of Lincoln University, he became the fourteenth president and the only Lincoln graduate to hold that position. As of this writing, he remains the only alumnus to become president of Lincoln University. During his tenure at Lincoln, he also served as secretary-treasurer and president of the NCAA. He was the first Black and the first college president to serve as NCAA president.

Lincoln University sets high on a hill in the Capitol City.

He was forty-two years old, the second-youngest president in Lincoln University history, when he left the president's home early one morning to drive the short distance to the campus to begin his first day on the job. He had always been an early riser and believed in starting each day with specific goals and objectives. He remembered having a rush of feelings – disbelief, recollections, gratefulness, challenges, joy, optimism, fulfillment of his goals and objectives for Lincoln University, and the anticipation of meeting with the faculty, students, and staff.

As he continued his short drive to the campus to occupy the President's office, he recalled having learned the beautiful school song, "Lincoln O' Lincoln." He started humming that sentimental tune, and he remembered having gone through the Alpha Phi Alpha fraternity in his sophomore year, and then he started humming that tune. The many warm memories returned again and again. He was overwhelmed and energetically filled with optimism and enthusiasm. He felt this would indeed be a journey of a lifetime. As he exited his car and climbed the familiar steps he had climbed thousands of times as a student, professor, and basketball coach, he was just overwhelmed with emotions!

Could he just be dreaming? When he approached his office and was greeted by happy faculty and staff, he could not stop smiling and remembered feeling happy and grateful. That moment in time would be indelibly etched in his memory!

He was blessed to have an excellent and caring executive assistant named Mrs. Vivian Jones. She had served under the previous president and was still in place, so the transition was smooth. She was thorough, efficient, intelligent, organized, thoughtful, and professional. She served as executive assistant to the president during his tenure. She remained a lifelong friend.

When Dr. Frank's youngest son, Troy, was attending nursery school on the University campus, Dr. Frank would take him to the nursery before going to work. However, he always had to go by the office first and let Troy say good morning to Mrs. Jones because Troy insisted on seeing her every morning. She was an invaluable assistant and friend. Thank God for Mrs. Jones. Interestingly, when Dr. Frank was a freshman student at Lincoln University, he had worked as a student assistant under the supervision of Mr. Lucius Jones, an industrial arts teacher and husband of Mrs. Vivian Jones. It was not even imaginable at that time that one day his supervisor's wife would be Dr. Frank's executive assistant as president of the university. It was even less conceivable that he would become his former supervisor's president.

Leadership Team

He worked well with the governing board of curators, and they shared mutual respect. It was a Board that operated professionally and understood the rules of governance, and most importantly, they understood the role of the board. He has many pleasant memories about his days serving as Lincoln president. He also remembers many of the challenges he faced from the very beginning. One of the biggest challenges was untangling the situation with the university finances. He knew this area needed immediate and thorough attention. He fully understood that in many colleges and universities, their downfall began finances went awry. This happens too often in HBCUs for various reasons, one being that they must do so much with so little. He could not let the university become another victim of those circumstances. So, many of his energies were expended on evaluating the financial operations at the University, including reorganization, getting special reports, hiring new staff, ongoing monitoring of the situation, and initiating a successful Economic Impact Study. As a result of his leadership, there was a commendable turnaround in operations and results that created complete financial stability for the University. The improvements in many University operations became quite apparent.

When Dr. Frank became president of Lincoln, the following people served on the Lincoln University Board of Curators:[10]

President – James A. Randle, St. Louis, Missouri

Vice President – Bruce Normile, Edina, Missouri

Secretary – RB Doolin, Kansas City, Missouri

Treasurer – Effie M. Hughes, Springfield, Missouri

Carl F. Sapp, Columbia, Missouri

Joseph McDuffie, St. Louis, Missouri

Lewis W. Clymer, Kansas City, Missouri

Hal E. Hunter Jr., New Madrid, Missouri

He had to hire a team of people who would sit on the president's cabinet and become a part of his inner circle. Hiring took a lot of time and concerted effort. Eventually, after having completed the task, he felt confident that he had the right people in the correct positions. The cabinet members were John Chavis, L. R. Hughes, Addison Williams, Ted Wilson, Jessie Johnson, Vivian Jones, Al Ottley, and Deloris Lewis.

Meetings with the faculty and staff went smoothly. Some of the faculty members had been teaching at the University when Dr. Frank was a student. One of those persons was Dr. Thomas Pawley. Some who were no longer at the University were still living in Jefferson City: Dr. Carl Hardiman, Mr. Chick Pullam, Mr. Lucius Jones, and Dr. Lorenzo Greene, to name a few.

---

[10] Obtained from Lincoln University Archivist, Mark Schleer, 2018

Dr. Frank always believed in shared governance, so he instituted the Faculty Senate, which still exists today. He did not face any resistance from the faculty on the concept, which always makes life a little easier. When people are given opportunities for involvement in the decision-making process that affects them, they are more likely to cooperate and provide positive input. Dr. Frank had always adhered to the democratic process, and partly because of that, he had been very effective in leadership roles.

Other Aspects of Administration

The Homecoming that year was a huge success. Dr. Frank and his good friend Earl Wilson, president of the National Alumni Association, worked together. As a result, attendance was one of the highest in the history of the University at that time. That year, 1973, was often referred to as "The Year of The Big Homecoming." It was a joy to see old friends and alumni many of whom Dr. Frank had not seen since his days as a student, teacher, or coach. Meeting alums who preceded him or attended the University after him was also fun. In subsequent official communication with the alumni, Dr. Frank thanked them for returning in such large numbers.

Homecoming is a highly anticipated weekend for alumni, students, faculty, administration, and friends of the University. On Saturday morning during the Homecoming weekend, the Franks always hosted a luncheon for the alumni, and those luncheons were always well-attended. Many people came to renew old acquaintances, reminisce, offer congratulations, see the president's residence, and visit for various other reasons. Many came because they were former classmates or students of Mr. and Mrs. Frank or knew them through some other channel. However, those weekends remain in memory as thoroughly enjoyable for the Frank family and attendees.

After a few years, it became difficult at times for the Franks to categorize alumni - sometimes having to recall whether the person was a former classmate or student, someone they had known previously, or an individual they had met for the first time during one of the Homecoming weekends. The Franks often laughed when that happened. Hundreds of former students returned during Dr. Frank's first year as president partly because he and the National Alumni president, Earl Wilson, had urged the participation partly due to the excitement surrounding the fact that Dr. Frank was the first alum to become President. In a mass mailing of the Alumni Bulletin sent to alumni following Homecoming, the words from the president emblazoned across the front cover were "We Asked You to Come Back, and You Did." That was a great Homecoming. During Dr. Frank's tenure, many alumni chapters were reactivated, and many new chapters were formed.

Drs. James and Zelma Frank with Earl Wilson (left) and Andrew Young (Right) at a Lincoln University Alumni Convention in Atlanta, GA.

Getting ready for graduation and the conferring of degrees was something Dr. Frank had not yet done as President. In the spring of 1974, he looked forward to that ceremonial occasion. He conferred degrees upon 394 students, and in the Summer of that year, 122 students graduated. On both occasions, graduation was flawless, and once again, he could not stop smiling. He was pleased that the planning and preparation were so successful and proud to be leading so many young men and women through the educational portals through which he had once passed.

As with her husband, "Pomp and Circumstance" had always been one of Dr. Zelma Frank's favorite musical renditions, first played in the United States in 1906 at Yale's commencement. It is now played at almost every graduation ceremony in America. Mrs. Frank always enjoyed graduations, so along with her other duties, she looked forward to the one that required her to attend the yearly graduation ceremonies. Having graduated as a Lincoln alumna added even more depth to the experience for her. Little did she know when she graduated that she would once again march to that song. Five years later, in 1979, she received her Ed.D. degree from the University of Missouri, Columbia, and graduates marched into the auditorium to the tune of "Pomp and Circumstance." That is still one of Mrs. Frank's favorite musical selections. The occasion was made even more special by the fact that Mrs. Frank was selected as the class marshall for the ceremony.

Other annual events that the couple thoroughly enjoyed hosting were the Christmas dinner for the board of curators and their spouses, the yearly dinner given for the retired professors and their spouses, the Homecoming Alumni Luncheon, and the fall reception for entering first-year students. The Christmas dinner for the Lincoln University board of curators was always a joyful occasion. It was usually scheduled for one evening during the first week of December, so it kicked off the holiday season and set the stage for other celebrations in December.

The Franks hosted the dinner at the president's residence, catered by the University Food Service. There were menu planners who consulted with Mrs. Frank, people who brought the food to the house, cooks, servers, hosts, a cleanup crew, and everything necessary for an excellent guest experience and a carefree evening for Mrs. Frank. What a life!

*Drs. James and Zelma Frank at a reception at the
Lincoln University president's residence in 1975*

It should be noted here that Troy, the youngest son who was three years old at the time, always looked forward to dressing up and helping his parents host every event held at the house. His presence and assistance added an unusual and delightful touch. He made his parents proud, and they were delighted with his motivation, at such a young age, to assist in hosting the celebrations. That little boy is now Dr. Troy Frank, a tenured professor at Lincoln University.

The annual dinner given for the retired professors was equally enjoyable and done in the same manner as described above for the board of curators. When planning the menu, in collaboration with the chefs, the Franks paid attention to appropriate food choices in deference to the ages of the professors. All meals were catered by the University Food Service. The service was very efficient, and the food was consistently delicious! The retired professors always looked forward to the dinner and were very grateful. Some of those professors had been Dr. and Mrs. Frank's former teachers. That was fun!

The fall reception for entering the first-year students was one the Frank family always looked forward to with great anticipation, and the freshmen did also. All entering freshmen were invited to the president's residence for a reception/cookout. The Franks always lightheartedly and enthusiastically welcomed the students, but not without Dr. Frank's usual speech to the students about his high expectations for them and his open-door policy. Students introduced themselves, spoke briefly about where they were from, and identified their major and minor studies. Then the real party began. There was a wide variety of foods and beverages. The reception was always a high-spirited affair. There was dancing to the beat of live music or student disc jockeys. There was an open mike for students who wanted to showcase their talents. All of this took place on the wide driveway and extended patio in the back of the president's home, which sat on the top of a hill overlooking the highway (Interstate 50) to the left and the campus to the right. The view from the back of the president's home was magnificent!

The Franks always enjoyed that occasion. The only mishap during those fun-filled get-togethers was the time when one of the student disc jockeys forgot to bring his speaker to the house and had to borrow one from Dr. Frank's intricate stereo system. The volume exceeded the speaker's capacity, and as a result, the speaker "blew out!" Dr. Frank just took it in stride and always laughed about it whenever he recalled that event.

*Drs. James and Zelma Frank at the Lincoln University
President's Inauguration Ball*

The Inauguration

The inauguration on April 6, 1974, marking Dr. Frank's first year as president, was just incredible. The celebration was spread over several days and was superb in every respect. The Inaugural Convocation was held on Thursday, the Inaugural Concert on Friday, and the Inaugural Breakfast, and the program were held Saturday. The convocation was uplifting. The choir sang with anointing. The breakfast was delicious, and the program included music by the University String Ensemble which dedicated selections to Mrs. Frank. The program participants delivered powerful and inspiring speeches and presentations. The Inauguration Ball was meticulously planned and executed. If there ever was a perfect three-day celebration, that was it indeed. The atmosphere was full of jubilation. Thank God for those indelible celebratory moments in time!

During Dr. Frank's memorable, inspiring, and prophetic inaugural address, he said, "I wish to cite one of my favorite quotations. 'I am only one. but I am one. I do not do everything, but I can do something. What I can do, I ought to do, and what I ought to do by the grace of God, I will do.'" During his tenure at the helm, his accomplishments were numerous because he did what he ought to have done.

Family, Friends, and Far Away Places

In addition to all of the responsibilities that Dr. Frank had, he never once took his role as husband and father for granted. He was an attentive, loving, thoughtful husband and father. He loved his family. Dr. Frank beamed with pride when he attended his wife's graduation and watched as she received her doctorate from the University of Missouri-Columbia. His support, love, encouragement, and presence played a major role in ensuring the success of that venture. His contributions toward that accomplishment were immeasurable. After getting her degree, Dr. Frank worked at Lincoln University as Director of the reading center, and also taught undergraduate and graduate courses.

*At the University of Missouri (Columbia) commencement when
Zelma Frank received her doctorate in 1979*

Dr. Frank had a deep love and respect for family and friends, feelings that were displayed often in a variety of ways. He visited his family and his wife's family as frequently as possible, and those visits were reciprocal. He and his wife traveled thousands of miles, quite often, between Kansas City, Missouri, Aliquippa, Pennsylvania, and Toronto, Canada to visit their families and his surrogate family. He went on many trips to share time with friends, and they were always welcome to visit with him and his wife.

"Far Away Places" was one of Dr. Frank's favorite songs. His trip to Paris reminded him of the many faraway places that he often dreamed about as a little boy growing up in Aliquippa, Pennsylvania. Dr. and Mrs. Frank visited Earl and Marjorie Wilson, former classmates at Lincoln, who were living in Paris. Mr. Wilson, employed by IBM, was on assignment there in a very high-level administrative position. As mentioned earlier, he was the first person to inform Dr. Frank about the presidential job opening at Lincoln University and encouraged him to apply. During his tenure as president, Dr. Frank became involved with the National Collegiate Athletic Association (NCAA).

*Drs. James and Zelma Frank (left) with Earl and
Marjorie Wilson in Paris*

Chapter 7

At The Top of His Game – President, National Collegiate Athletic Association (NCAA)

While still serving as president of Lincoln, Dr. Frank was elected president of the NCAA, the first African American and first college president in that post. This achievement brought prestige to Lincoln University, HBCUs, and all NCAA Division II schools.
Mr. Victor Pasley,
President, Lincoln University Board of Curators
Frank Hall Unveiling ceremony, April 21, 2023.

Throughout his memorable career, Dr. Frank spearheaded positive and impactful change, championing diversity and inclusion in college sports.
Mark Emmert, Executive Director, NCAA

In many ways, the overriding issues or problems in athletics are not educational, physical, or economic, but more moral than anything else. It is about what we do right for our student-athletes and fellow human beings.
James Frank - Remarks made at NCAA National Convention in San Diego, California, 1982

Dr. Frank's legacy, I think, was not being afraid to step up on some sensitive and critical issues. During the early 80's and late '70s, we were going through a difficult time accepting women in collegiate sports, and I think Jim was a strong leader in providing direction for the NCAA.
Cedric Dempsey, Third Executive Director of the National Collegiate Athletic Association (NCAA) 1988-1993

Dr. James Frank is a legend. His contributions to intercollegiate athletics will be forever celebrated. Dr. Frank's commitment and dedication to the NCAA as a membership organization is an important part of his legacy, and the NCAA and the MIAA are grateful for his service and leadership.

Mike Racy, Commissioner, Michigan Intercollegiate Athletic Association (MIAA)

Dr. James Frank presiding at an NCAA Convention as the first African American and the first college president to serve as President of the NCAA

During his second year as president of Lincoln University, a friend's invitation to get involved with the National Collegiate Athletic Association (NCAA) shaped the course of college sports. The NCAA is "the nation's biggest and most influential governing body in college athletics."[11] It is also the most powerful and prestigious organization in college sports. Being affiliated with college sports, having worked with NCAA programs throughout his career, and leading teams to NCAA championships, Dr. Frank frequently attended the annual NCAA conventions. After he became president of Lincoln University, he continued to attend the conventions. Lincoln had an institutional membership in the NCAA which provided the impetus to continue his association with the organization. However, not many college presidents attended the annual conventions. That responsibility was commonly given to the athletics directors or faculty athletic representatives at each university.

The NCAA Council

At the annual convention in 1974, Dr. Frank was asked, by a long-time friend and former classmate at Springfield College, Mr. Stan Marshall, to serve on the NCAA Council. The Council was the highest governing body of the Association and consisted of the president, secretary-treasurer, and executive committee. The Council also managed the committees that set the course for the organization and made policy guidance and legislative recommendations to the membership. The entire membership either

---

[11] Atlanta Journal Constitution, Nov. 8, 2021

approved or disapproved all primary legislation. Membership on the Council was highly selective. The Council was the predecessor to the current NCAA governing body, the Board of Governors.

In 1975, Dr. Frank reluctantly agreed to serve after asking about the time commitments and other requirements. He reasoned that the time involved would not weigh too heavily and would be manageable in light of all his other responsibilities as president of Lincoln University. Well, the time and commitment involved in being a member of this very prestigious council far exceeded his wildest imaginings. The time commitment was greater than his friend had conveyed.

Although more time was required than Dr. Frank expected, he remained steadfast in his commitment and enjoyed serving on the Council. In retrospect, he was convinced that was one of the best decisions he had ever made. His commitment to serving on the NCAA Council was the beginning of a long, dedicated, meaningful, and historical involvement with the NCAA. Mr. Stan Marshall and Dr. Frank worked together as NCAA cohorts for many years and remained good friends until Stan passed away. His death touched Dr. Frank deeply.

While serving on the Council, he met Dr. Gwendolyn Norrell who later became one of his best friends and greatest supporters. She was the faculty representative from Michigan State University. She and Dr. Frank's youngest son, Troy, struck up a genuine friendship and mutual respect. She invited him to spend a few summers on the Michigan State campus where he attended summer basketball and tennis camps. After the three summers and Gwen's coaching, Troy enrolled at Michigan State. Four years later, he graduated from MSU and credited Gwen for many of his successes. Dr. Gwen Norrell affectionately called *"Doc"* and Dr. Frank established a SWAC scholarship named the Frank/Norrell Scholarship. It is awarded to a student from one of the SWAC Universities who seeks to pursue a master's degree in physical education or a related field.

After becoming a council member, Dr. Frank heard many college presidents complain that the athletics directors were wielding too much power in the organization. They pretty much had autonomy. Their decisions were not consistently in sync with those of the university presidents. Dr. Frank reasoned that if the presidents were dissatisfied, they should become more involved so he pushed for a change in representation. Through Council channels, he was able to convince the college presidents their involvement in the NCAA was of utmost importance and they should be the voice of their institutions. As a result of his efforts, influence, and convictions, a president's commission was established. The commission made recommendations to the Council and participated more freely in the discussions at the annual meetings. Through that commission, the presidents and chancellors were given a forum that enabled them to influence major policy issues relating to college athletics at all member institutions. The commission operated effectively and grew in significance. According to the NCAA archives, and Joe Crowley's book, *In the Arena: The NCAA's First Century*, in 1984 the presidents commission was officially ratified by the NCAA[12] , and became the "group of presidents from the three divisions charged with setting the agenda for the Association."[13]

College presidents continue their involvement in the NCAA governance from the highest-level board of governors which consists primarily of presidents and chancellors down through the Division I Board of Directors and the Division II & III Presidents Councils. Therefore, presidents and chancellors continue to make significant decisions affecting their universities and the rulings that affect the entire national community of colleges and universities.

The role of the athletics directors is still essential, but they are no longer the ultimate voice for their universities. That change marked a crucial turning point in the organizational structure and function of the NCAA in a very positive way. That is one of the significant structural changes attributed to Dr. Frank's influence as a member of the Council and the first college president to lead the organization.

Perhaps one of the most significant matters during that time was how the stage was being set for the future decision to integrate women's sports fairly and completely into NCAA intercollegiate athletics. Signed into law in 1972, "Title IX, the federal law prohibiting sex discrimination in education, led to an expansion of women's athletics programs at colleges and universities around the

---

[12] Joe Crowley, *In the Arena: The NCAA's First Century* (Indianapolis, NCAA, 2005)
[13] "Growth," NCAA, Accessed March 1, 2022, https://www.ncaa.org/sports/2021/5/4/history.aspx:

country in the 1970s."[14] "The passage of Title IX produced programmatic, personnel, and structural changes on a large scale."[15] Dr. Frank and others felt strongly that the NCAA had to proactively address this issue and he led the governance committee in developing a strategic plan. He would later implement that plan during his tenure as president.

This was just the beginning, as Dr. Frank would continue to make a difference through his tremendous contributions to the National Collegiate Athletic Association.   While he served as president of Lincoln University from 1973 until 1983, he remained actively involved in the NCAA through his eventual election as its president. He served on the NCAA Council from January 1975 until January 1983. He was still considered a member of the Council during his tenure as secretary-treasurer and president.

Secretary-Treasurer

Having served on the NCAA Council for two years and observing how the organization functioned, Dr. Frank decided he would like to be president of the NCAA because he saw the need for changes and felt very strongly that he could continue to make significant contributions. He started working toward accomplishing that goal. Voting took place during the NCAA Annual Convention in San Francisco in 1979.

---

[14] "Growth," NCAA, Accessed March 1, 2022, https://www.ncaa.org/sports/2021/5/4/history.aspx:
[15] Crowley, Arena, iii

At the annual convention, when the election committee met and the voting took place to elect the President, he felt that he should have won the election and was very disappointed when he did not. The election committee voted many times, each vote culminating in a tie. The committee decided that if there were another tie, the matter would have to be taken to the convention floor for the entire membership to cast votes. When the subsequent vote took place, someone changed his or her vote, and Dr. Frank lost by one vote.

The person with the second highest number of votes became secretary-treasurer which was a two-year term like that of the president. He was that person; however, looking through the veil of disappointment, he had some trepidation about accepting that position. Clarence "Big House" Gaines, a friend and long-time legendary Naismith Basketball Hall of Fame coach at Winston Salem State University in South Carolina, a committee member, encouraged him to accept the position. However, he was still not convinced, so he continued to waver. He called his wife and relayed what had happened and asked for her opinion about whether he should accept. Her simple yet thought-provoking question consisted of only two words, "Why Not?"

He accepted the position of secretary-treasurer, the first college president to hold that position. The report from the elections committee was then presented to the entire membership. The vote to accept Mr. Bill Flynn as President and Dr. James Frank as Secretary-Treasurer was unanimous; consequently, Bill Flynn and Dr. Frank became very close friends. Their families spent many happy and memorable hours together. The two leaders worked together well as a team, and in close circles, were sometimes referred to as the "Flynn/Frank Team." Those two years were filled with many enriching experiences.

Dr. Frank served as secretary-treasurer from January 1979 to January 1981. During his tenure as secretary-treasurer, he was the influential chairman of the Special Committee on NCAA Governance which addressed the issues dealing with the inclusion of women's sports into the NCAA. "The Frank Committee included four presidents, four faculty representatives, four athletics directors, and one conference commissioner. Two of the members were women."[16] The problems were long-standing, dating back to the years before he got on the NCAA Council. Together with staff and working alongside Dr. Gwen Norrell, his good friend and faculty representative from Michigan State University, he traveled throughout the country conducting conferences, asking questions, researching the issues involved, and reaching consensus on sensitive, sometimes volatile issues. Having been involved in the sports arena for so many years, Dr. Frank was very knowledgeable about the overall issues and some of the underlying emotional challenges for both men and women.

In the words of Joseph Crowley, author of *In the Arena; the NCAA's First Century*, "The NCAA's first 75 years ended, and the next quarter-century began, with a historic decision to bring women's sports into the Association fold. The action both symbolically and substantively introduced the modern era for intercollegiate athletics and the organization that governs them. The

---

[16] Crowley, Arena, iv

committee that recommended the action was chaired by a member institution chief executive, James Frank, who in the same year (1981) was chosen as the NCAA's first African American president."[17] Dr. Frank's impactful leadership and influence continued throughout the whole process. He felt very strongly that women's sports should be included, not excluded.

President

At that time, the president was elected by a vote of the entire NCAA membership, through the election committee, at the annual convention. The presidency was a non-salaried elected two-year position. The full-time, salaried executive director was responsible for the day-to-day operations and management of the organization. Today that same salaried position is titled, "president." To differentiate and add clarity, the position that Dr. Frank held is sometimes referred to as "membership president." The role of the former elected position of president is now filled by the Chair of the Governance Council and remains a two-year elected position where that person heads the membership. The historical background regarding nomenclature can be found in Joe Crowley's book which reads as follows:

> Major developments within the first 100 years have had an impact on NCAA nomenclature. One significant adjustment, for instance, is the title of the NCAA's Chief Executive Officer. Byers was appointed in 1951 to the newly created position of executive director. In the wake of the mid-1990s

---

[17] Crowley, *Arena*, iv

restructuring, the chief executive designation was changed to President. The title, until then, had been held since 1906 by individuals from the membership whose terms were defined (usually 2 years), whose service was voluntary and whose office was roughly equivalent to that of a corporation's Chairman of the Board. Byers (1951-87) and Richard Schultz (1987-93) were executive directors. Cedric Dempsey was appointed to that position in 1994, but his title changed to president in 1998. Myles Brand, the current president, began his service in 2003. Before 1998, 31 men and one woman, all volunteers, filled the position of NCAA President. That position is now often referred to as "Membership President.[18]

Dr. Frank did not know that he would become president because it was not an automatic transition. The voting procedure for president had to occur. When the secret ballot voting took place for president, at the 1981 NCAA Annual Convention in Miami, Florida, he won the election by unanimous consent and would serve the two-year term. Again, his election as the president made him the first African American, the first college president, and the first individual from a Division II college to hold the position. His presidency represented a defining moment in NCAA history. He had a significant influence on the decision-making process that shaped the history of college sports, and the lives of college athletes.

---

[18] Crowly, Arena, iv

He was President of the NCAA from January 1981 to January 1983. While serving as President of the NCAA, he was involved in many issues, and his influence and leadership resulted in changes that altered the landscape of intercollegiate athletics. "Under his leadership, many changes occurred. He presided over the passing of the controversial Proposition 48, which set eligibility standards for student-athletes who were freshmen. Students were required to have a 2.0 minimum GPA, a 700 score on the SAT, and 11 core classes. Under Proposition 48 regulations, graduation rates for student-athletes increased. This was not the expectation of many individuals opposed to Proposition 48, particularly some African American coaches and administrators. Many African Americans felt that the higher requirements would have a negative impact on the number of Black first-year college students eligible to participate in sports. "Controversy aside, Proposition 48, establishing for students an academic basis for their eligibility to compete, was an effort to reinsert the importance of that historic connection."[19]

As mentioned earlier, Dr. Frank was very instrumental in incorporating women's sports into the NCAA hierarchy. His actions and his influence were critical. The challenges were many but not insurmountable. Among the many roadblocks was the opinion of many female leaders who felt that joining such a large, powerful entity as the NCAA would lessen their influence, and they would become buried in the process. These leaders felt that remaining separate from the NCAA and obtaining resources equivalent to those of their \male counterparts would be more advantageous.

---

[19] Crowley, Arena, 65

Again, Dr. Frank was unequivocal in his conviction that women should be included within the NCAA structure. "Frank's view on this matter was emphatic. It was in part a product of his own experience. He stated, "I think it is fallacious thinking… that separate but equal is the answer. I, for one, know that separate but equal does not lead to equality."[20]

The women's organization at that time was the Association for Intercollegiate Athletics for Women (AIAW), and members were self-governed. Some women did not want to lose this distinction. Some men were also opposed to the idea of incorporating women's sports into the NCAA. Nevertheless, Dr. Frank stressed and pushed forward with his position stating that "Title IX made it clear that you should make provisions for women in your organization."

According to information available on the internet, "the AIAW was founded in 1971 to govern collegiate women's athletics in the United States and administer national championships. It evolved out of the Commission on Intercollegiate Athletics for women. The Association was one of the most significant advancements for women's athletics at the collegiate level. Throughout the 1970s, the AIAW increased in membership and influence, parallel with the national growth of women's sports following the enactment of Title IX. The AIAW functioned in the equivalent role for college women's programs that the National Collegiate Athletic Association had done for men's programs. Owing to its success, the AIAW was in a

---

[20] Crowley, Arena, 131

vulnerable position that precipitated conflicts with the NCAA in the early 1980s. Following a one-year overlap in which both organizations staged women's championships, the AIAW discontinued operation. Most member schools continued their women's athletic programs under the governance of the NCAA."

As a member of the Council, Dr. Frank chaired the governance subcommittee which composed the overall plan that determined how and when women's championship games would be included in the structure of the NCAA. In 1981, his first year as president, the NCAA adopted the plan and "Added 19 Women's Championships, including Division 1 and National Collegiate events. In November of 1981, the first women's teams were crowned NCAA champions, ushering in a new era for women's sports."[21] This has been referred to as the most significant change in NCAA history. Dr. Frank stated, "The schools had to open up their pocketbooks and start spending money on women's sports. I certainly thought it was the right thing to do, so it made it easier."[22]

Some other very tough issues ensued, one of which was the uneven distribution of television funds between the large and small schools. This disparity and some schools wanting to negotiate their own television contracts developed into an issue of property rights. The hotly debated conflict had to be resolved at a special NCAA Convention, presided over by Dr. Frank. The NCAA was

---

[21] "Growth," NCAA, Accessed March 1, 2022,
https://www.ncaa.org/sports/2021/5/4/history.aspx:
[22] "Growth," NCAA, Accessed March 1, 2022,
https://www.ncaa.org/sports/2021/5/4/history.aspx:

responsible for all television negotiations, and his involvement and leadership during those proceedings were crucial. Today, schools and conferences negotiate their contracts.

Pictured with legendary news anchor Walter Cronkite at the
1982 NCAA Theodore Roosevelt Award ceremony during
Dr. Frank's term as NCAA President

College and NCAA budgetary issues were sometimes challenging but manageable. Title IX Lawsuits filed by the University of Georgia and the University of Oklahoma and numerous other lawsuits were filed while Dr. Frank was President.

He had the major leadership role in establishing the NCAA Minority Opportunities and Interest Committee. This committee was charged with ensuring minority inclusion in NCAA policy decisions. The committee not only still exists today but exercises major influence in the policy decisions and legislation of the entire organization. Dr. Frank's influence is reflected in the following paragraph which also includes his impact on increasing the inclusion of women.

During his tenure as president, women received guaranteed positions on all NCAA committees. "Frank supported the legislation guaranteeing certain numbers of positions for females. But he asked to have a statement about another under-represented group included in the 1981 Convention program. It read in part: 'The association should commit itself to a concerted effort to provide opportunities for Blacks and other minorities to hold viable roles in [its] administrative structure.' Plenty of work remained to be done in honoring that commitment."[23]

He facilitated and enhanced presidential collaboration through the NCAA Long-Range Planning Committee, leading to a more diverse demographic change in Association leadership. He was a significant influence in shaping college sports as he led the organization through an arduous time of making many effective decisions regarding substantial changes. Dr. Frank served on many important committees, including the Walter Byers Scholarship Committee which he chaired.

The challenges of being President sometimes emanated from unexpected occurrences outside of normal policy issues. While serving as president of the NCAA, he remembered very well one riveting experience on March 30, 1981. During the weekend of the Final Four Championship Games in Philadelphia, Pennsylvania, an attempt was made to assassinate the fortieth President of the United States, Ronald Reagan. John Hinckley Jr. shot Reagan and three other people as they left the Washington Hilton Hotel in Washington, D. C. Dr. Frank, along with other high-ranking

---

[23] Crowley, Arena, 131

officials in the Organization, had to convene and decide whether or not to cancel the Monday night championship game between the University of Louisville and UCLA. After hours of emotional and laborious discussion, the decision was made to continue the games. Being involved in that decision-making process was unsettling.

He addressed the issues with dignity and aplomb. He was always knowledgeable, articulate, and convincing. He could coordinate and negotiate and bring opposing sides together at the table and discuss heated and controversial issues without raising resentment and disrespect among members. Those leadership skills sometimes earned him the nickname "A Man for All Seasons." He will long be remembered for his many contributions in the above areas and his overall contributions to the NCAA.

Summary of Accomplishments

At the culmination of his five years of council leadership and his two-year term as NCAA president, it can be stated unequivocally that "during Dr. Frank's presidency, he was a significant influence in defining NCAA decisions:

1. Dr. Frank chaired the governance subcommittee and oversaw the governance plan that defined how and when women's sports and championships would become part of the NCAA.

2. Dr. Frank presided over the passing of Proposition 48, the legislation that set eligibility standards for incoming freshman student-athletes, which resulted in raising graduation rates.

3. Dr. Frank facilitated enhanced presidential collaboration through the NCAA Long-Range Planning Committee which led to a demographic change in Association leadership.

4. Dr. Frank was integral in the NCAA's establishment of the Minority Opportunities and Interest Committee, a group devoted to inclusiveness in Association policy decisions."[24]

5. Dr. Frank was instrumental in increasing the level of presidential involvement in the NCAA governance process by beginning the President's Commission during his leadership tenure.

Dr. James Frank's history is next to the conference room, which bears his name at the NCAA National Headquarters, Indianapolis, IN

---

[24] "First Black NCAA President, Dr. James Frank has Died," HBCU Buzz Reporters, Last Modified January 28, 2019 - https://hbcubuzz.com/2019/01/first-black-ncaa-president-dr-james-frank-has-died/.

A fitting recognition was an honor bestowed upon him in 2013 when he was asked for his permission to name a room after him in the National NCAA Headquarters in Indianapolis, Indiana. Mrs. Frank recalls how deeply humbled he was when he received that request. The Frank Room had been there for many years, and during the NCAA Final Four weekend in 2015, the NCAA hosted a ceremony for the unveiling of his picture which now hangs in the room. He has also been recognized in other ways by the NCAA for his stellar leadership. During the NCAA Centennial Celebration, the NCAA listed Dr. Frank among the "100 Most Influential Student-Athletes During the Past 100 Years." The list is widely distributed and publicized.

Dr. James Frank and Dr. Cedric Dempsey, former NCAA President,
and Executive Director at the picture unveiling ceremony

On January 12, 2008, at the NCAA National Convention in Nashville, Tennessee, he was awarded the prestigious Gerald R.

Ford Award. The award, named for the thirty-eighth president of the United States, is given yearly to honor a person who the NCAA describes as an "individual who has provided significant leadership as an advocate for intercollegiate athletics throughout their career." At that time, Dr. Myles Brand was President of the NCAA, and his words eloquently reflected Dr. Frank's life journey. Dr. Brand said, "At every stop along his career, from student-athlete to university president to his involvement in NCAA governance, Dr. James Frank has been a catalyst for important and positive change. For more than forty years, he has championed the values of diversity and inclusion within intercollegiate athletics. Dr. Frank holds a special place in NCAA history, serving as both the first African American and the first college president to hold the positions of secretary-treasurer and president."[25] Some past recipients of the Gerald R. Ford Award follow:

- 2004: Theodore Hesburgh
- 2005: William C. Friday
- 2006: Birch Bayh & John Wooden
- 2007: Christine Grant
- 2008: James Frank
- 2009: Billie Jean King
- 2010: Myles Brand
- 2011: Joe Paterno
- 2012: Pat Summitt
- 2013: Donna Lopiano

---

[25] From Myles Brand speech during Gerald R. Ford Award ceremony 1/12/2008

- 2014: James Andrews
- 2015: Walter Harrison
- 2016: Condoleezza Rice
- 2017: Grant Hill
- 2018: Robin Roberts
- 2019: Jackie Joyner-Kersee
- 2020: Dick Vital

It should be noted that was the only award Dr. Frank ever received when Mrs. Frank was not in attendance. She normally attended many NCAA National Conventions, including the ones over which her husband presided. On that occasion, she had traveled with her husband from their home in New Orleans, Louisiana, to Nashville, Tennessee, to see him receive the award at the convention. During that time, they were once again living in New Orleans, having returned after Hurricane Katrina. One day after getting to Nashville, Mrs. Frank was hospitalized with pneumonia and missed the ceremony scheduled for the following day. She remained in the hospital for one week. However, Dr. Frank's two sons, two grandchildren, other relatives, and friends were there including Nichelle Gainey, a very good friend, and former SWAC administrator. A niece and nephew, Mishi and Terry Esper were also in attendance. Dr. and Mrs. Frank felt that the necessity for hospitalization and missing the award ceremony was somewhat unbelievable.

Impactful Experiences

During his presidency at Lincoln University, Dr. Frank's involvement with the NCAA generated many memorable experiences. Dr. and Mrs. Frank attended the 1980 Winter Olympics in Lake Placid, New York. Of course, one of the most exciting parts of this experience was being in the arena on February 22, 1980, and witnessing the "Miracle on Ice" when the US hockey team defeated the Russians in a 4-3 upset in the semi-finals, classified by ESPN as the greatest American sports moment of the twentieth century. The hockey game between the United States and Russia was one to remember! That entire trip experience was just awesome in every respect, including the royal treatment received from beginning to end.

*Drs. James and Zelma at the 1980 Winter Olympics
in Lake Placid, New York*

Another very meaningful and unforgettable experience was when Dr. Frank was asked, as president of the NCAA, to escort the top student golfers from colleges throughout the United States to a competition in Japan. The golf tournament was known as Japan vs the United States. That was the eighth Annual College Golf Match and took place December 15 through 17, 1982. Mrs. Frank accompanied Dr. Frank and the golfers on the trip and walked the eighteen-hole golf course every day of the tournament. The Franks thoroughly enjoyed the experience, got to know the students well, and had excellent travel plans, meals, accommodations, and interpreters. Dr. Zelma Frank and their primary interpreter remain friends and still correspond today. The opportunity to escort young college athletes to Japan and watch them compete against young Japanese college athletes was special. That was an awesome experience that will always remain in the top tier of outstanding and extraordinary events for Dr. and Mrs. Frank. Two of those student golfers later became professional golfers, and Dr. Frank followed their careers. He had the opportunity to talk with one of them, Brad Faxon, during the height of his career, and they reminisced about the trip to Japan. Faxon won eight times on the PGA Tour and later became a television golf analyst. Those are such special moments to remember and another "faraway place" to embrace!

Attending the NCAA Final Four Basketball Championship Games was always enjoyable, and the Franks looked forward to it with great anticipation. Watching their son, Troy, perform as a ball boy during many of those games added to the fun. The Franks attended the NCAA Final Four Men's Basketball Championship

Tournaments for thirty-six consecutive years. The continuity was disrupted beginning with the games in Phoenix, Arizona, in 2016.

Drs. James and Zelma Frank with NFL Legend Jim Brown, recipient of the NCAA Silver Anniversary Award, at the 1982 NCAA Theodore Roosevelt Award ceremony during Dr. Frank's term as NCAA President

Dr. Frank's involvement with the NCAA continued while he served as president of Lincoln University. His obligations were not in conflict. His responsibilities at Lincoln University were very important to him, and he prioritized them appropriately. He said, "I enjoyed my role as a teacher, coach, and college president tremendously. It offered me an opportunity to affect the lives of students and colleagues in a very positive way." He also commented, "It's been an honor and a blessing to serve and be involved in such a prestigious and powerful organization as the NCAA." In the book written by Joe Crowley, *In The Arena: The*

NCAA's First Century, Dr. Frank is acknowledged by the author for his "invaluable assistance" through the interview, and for having read one or more draft chapters."[26]

When assessing Dr. Frank's position as President of the NCAA, Lauren Kirschman states in the *Beaver County Times* newspaper article, March 13, 2016, titled "Layup decisions," "Former NCAA President, Aliquippa native left a mark. So many decisions came easily to James Frank. He didn't have to think about them. He didn't lose any sleep. Even the most significant calls – the ones that helped shape the dynamics of collegiate athletics – seemed simple, so long as he believed he was doing the right thing."[27] This statement reflects the principle by which Dr. Frank lived – do the right thing.

---

[26] Crowly, Arena, v.
[27] Lauren Kirschman, "Layup Decisions," Beaver County Times, March 13, 2016

Dr. James Frank presiding at an NCAA Convention (1979-1983) as the only African American and the first college president to serve as president of the NCAA

Chapter 8

Legacy, Integrity, And Departure from Lincoln

The effective leader must have the courage to be optimistic, the courage to make tough decisions, the courage to take a stand when in the minority, the courage to speak the truth, the courage to dare to be different, and the courage to walk to the beat of that other drummer. In addition to all of this, the effective moral leader must have the courage to do the right thing.
James Frank

He was a major influencer, and highly-respected higher education professional for many years. His name is a household word in higher education circles, which also includes collegiate athletics. (And) I have come to understand that one of his driving principles was his quest for excellence in all that he did. I understand that he was a man of integrity, who was committed to doing the right thing, no matter the cost.
Jerald Jones Woolfolk
20th President, Lincoln University

I believe today's renaming is a fitting tribute to a man whose life was a testimony of what it means to be a true Lincolnite. Our University oath reminds us to leave Lincoln better than it was when we arrived. Every time Dr. James Frank stepped on this campus, he made it better, and this renaming is in celebration of that.
Dr. John Mosley,
Twenty-First President of Lincoln University,
Remarks during the ceremony renaming Founders Hall to Frank Hall, April 21, 2023.

Dr. and Mrs. Frank pose with the Lincoln University Ambassadors he founded
circa 1980 to represent the University in their blue blazers with
the Lincoln logo. Dr. and Mrs. Frank are sixth and seventh from right.

D r. Frank's experiences as president of Lincoln University were challenging, but many accomplishments crowned his presidency. The years were memorable and rewarding and filled with a fantastic number of nostalgic moments. His accomplishments at Lincoln were historical, strategic, long-lasting, and essential. He thoroughly enjoyed the job of being president. Interacting with the students, faculty, and staff kept him highly motivated and energized.

Legacy

His accomplishments were many and varied, some of them follow:

1. The faculty organization was restructured and named the Faculty Senate.

2. Offices no longer were allowed to close during the lunch hour, eliminating the "all campus office shutdown hour."

3. He initiated the research that resulted in hiring a new food service.

4. He served on many NCAA committees and had important assignments that brought national recognition to Lincoln University.

5. He strengthened the ties between Lincoln University and the National Alumni Association. This work was done with the invaluable insight and cooperation of Mr. Earl Wilson, president of the National Alumni Association.

6. Dr. Frank was also successful in improving the relationship between Lincoln University and the Jefferson City community.

7. The signs on Highways 50 and 54, which direct motorists to Lincoln University, posted one of his accomplishments not easily done although they should have been. History, politics, and lack of cooperation from some decision-makers were opposing forces, which prolonged getting the signage accomplished. Looking at those signs today is rewarding and very much worth the efforts expended.

8. Shortly after assuming the presidency, he initiated fund-raising activities to build the new Memorial Hall Building on the site of the old Memorial Hall which was demolished. Funds for the building, a tribute to the University founders, were garnered through alumni, federal, and private sources. He was instrumental in obtaining a $125,000 challenge grant from the National Endowment for the Humanities for this effort. That resulted in a 3:1 matching grant. He raised a total of three hundred and seventy-five thousand dollars to match the grant.

9. The Music Association approved the music program for the first time in the history of the University.

10. Student enrollment increased by 4.2% from 1973 to 1983 through the Project 800 Student Recruitment Project.

11. The National Council for Accreditation of Teacher Education (NCATE) accredited the Teacher Education Program for the first time in the history of the University.

12. The University instituted sound financial planning and achieved complete financial stability.

13. The Fine Arts Center was completely renovated.

14. The Small Animal Research Facility was constructed in 1979.

15. The Utility Distribution System was constructed over the entire campus saving the University thousands of dollars monthly in utility costs.

16. The entire academic program was reorganized into three separate colleges, and the number of departments was reduced from twenty-three to twelve, resulting in savings of approximately $500,000.

17. The first Economic Impact Study for Lincoln University was completed.

18. The Tompkins Health Center was constructed.

19. The Shipping and Receiving Building was erected.

20. Significant renovations were made to the president's residence.

21. The reactivation of numerous LU Alumni chapters and the creation of new chapters was accomplished.

22. He instituted an "open door policy" for students, welcoming them to his office at any time. He also initiated an annual reception/ cookout for the entering freshman class held at the President's residence.

23. He initiated an annual dinner celebration for all of the Retired Lincoln University Professors and their spouses.

24. He instituted the Lincoln University Ambassadors Organization, composed of faculty and staff members, to represent and promote the university at various venues and social settings.

25. Dr. Frank Established a prison education program at the Missouri Penitentiary and Algoa Reformatory for Men (1973).

26. He instituted two new graduate degree programs: Master of Education in Adult Education (1973), and Master of Business Administration in Management (1974).

27. Benefits of the land-grant status were utilized to expand research projects and extension services which garnered respect throughout the state.

28. He established the Lincoln University Ethnic Studies Center housed in Inman E. Page Library.

29. He established offices for Veterans Affairs and International Students.

30. He created a specific budget for the Student Government Association.

31. The Lincoln University Foundation became a valuable asset to the University.

A portion of the Lincoln University campus with Jefferson City and the Missouri State Capital building in the background

While serving as President of Lincoln University, Dr. Frank was appointed by United States President Richard M. Nixon, to serve on the board of Visitors for the United States military academies. This board was responsible for evaluating the athletic programs at all the service academies. Having served on the Board, he was invited to attend Army/Navy football games. He and his wife attended one of those games, and the experience was ever so great.

Dr. Frank also served on the Board for Blue Cross Blue Shield Insurance. This appointment entailed travels to St. Louis, Missouri, for Board Meetings. He found this to be a very thought-provoking and enlightening experience.

Regarding Dr. Frank's tenure, in words on a display in the library, Mark Schleer, University Archivist, penned the following:

> He did it ALL for Lincoln University. A student, alumnus, instructor, coach, and finally, President. Frank served his alma mater in nearly every possible capacity. His tenure at Lincoln was memorable and inspiring. The growth of the university during his administration was phenomenal and he certainly made his fellow Lincolnites proud by serving as the only Lincoln graduate to become President of the institution.
>
> Dr. Frank was a pioneer in the world of college athletics, serving as the first African American President of the National Collegiate Athletic Association; a position that the former Blue Tiger basketball standout cherished deeply. His willingness to serve, devotion to his family, and dedication to his alma mater are just a few of the many attributes for which Dr. Frank will

be remembered, but, most of all, he will be reckoned as a compassionate man.[28]

Integrity

Dr. Frank experienced some tough moments at Lincoln University. One particularly challenging and grueling situation was the ongoing court appearances to contest the discrimination lawsuit against the University by a Caucasian professor. The lawsuit had been filed before Dr. Frank was appointed President. Because of her interest in the case and to support her husband, Mrs. Frank was in court every day. Thanks to the unyielding efforts of two very competent lawyers, Lincoln won the case. That victory led to a grand celebration at the president's residence.

One of the most challenging personal and emotional moments at Lincoln University for Dr. Frank was removing a very good long-time friend from the position of Head Football Coach. He was also a Pennsylvania native and close enough in friendship for Dr. Frank's sons to call him "Uncle." He was instrumental in Jim's going back to Lincoln earlier in his career as a coach and instructor and later in his decision to seek a master's degree at Springfield College. They both served simultaneously in the Army, even visiting each other in Korea. Dr. Frank hired him as the new football coach, but over his four seasons as head coach, his win/loss record had raised the ire of fans, alumnae, and the board of curators. By the end of his fourth

---

[28] Written by Lincoln University Archivist, Mark Schleer for The James Frank Display at Inman E. Page Library, Lincoln University

season, the record was 6-36-2, only compiling six wins over his four years as head coach.

Dr. Frank knew that a change was inevitable; additionally, the board of curators was very vocal in their insistence that termination was in order. Because of their long friendship and his friend's sincerity and love for Lincoln, termination was a heart-wrenching idea. Dr. Frank spent long hours trying to make the most objective, fair, and humane decision. He gave his friend the option to resign. His friend chose not to quit.

Dr. Frank had the compassion to hire him in another position. Firing him and leaving him jobless, even for a moment, was just not Dr. Frank's best option. He hired him as athletics director, a vacant, high-level administrative position for which he was well qualified. As a result, the coach was able to continue working at Lincoln. Later, Dr. Frank also made the professional decision to hire the new athletics director's wife as director of alumni affairs, where she did an outstanding job. Making tough decisions is a part of administrative leadership which is sometimes very difficult and painful. He always sought to be humane and objective which afforded him a degree of comfort in the decision-making process.

The most challenging time for Dr. Frank was when he encountered deep philosophical, organizational, professional, and ethical disagreements with the board of curators as the board membership changed from the one in place when he was hired. Following the dictates of some of the board members would not have been in the best interest of his alma mater, Lincoln University. He was unwilling to sacrifice principle, honesty, and integrity even at the risk of losing his job. Had he been willing to follow the dictates of the board, his sojourn at Lincoln would have ended differently. He harbored absolutely no regrets about the decisions and the actions he took.

The final chapter for Dr. Frank as president of Lincoln University began to reveal itself two or three years before he submitted his resignation letter. As college presidents know, when the board of curators changes, with new appointments, so does the mixture of personalities, agendas, goals, objectives, politics, and the understanding of member roles. Dr. Frank's goals for the University, methods, philosophy, and overall logical, proper, and legal operating procedures were sometimes in conflict with several of the most vocal board members. Those members, in turn, had a negative influence on some of the other Board Members.

Dr. Frank, a highly principled and honest individual, was unwilling to sacrifice his beliefs and knowledge regarding proper and legal college administration and what was in the best interest of his alma mater, was unwilling to act in opposition to what he knew was right. As a result, he became less favored by several of the most vocal board members, who unfortunately misunderstood their roles and severely lacked knowledge about college administration. Some of the most vocal board members were bent on micromanaging and trying to convince Dr. Frank to do things that were in direct contrast to sound administrative principles and would have been detrimental to the University, faculty, and students.

This situation was not an unusual occurrence because it happens when some college and university boards when board members do not clearly understand their roles. Unfortunately, this is a severe matter that often goes unaddressed and results in college presidents leaving their posts or being asked to leave. The writer's observation is that it appears to happen all too frequently. The Association of Governing Boards (AGB) addresses the role of college governing boards at their meetings, annual conventions, and in articles in their publications. Some means of required orientation for board members would probably prove to be beneficial.

Departure

As the differences escalated between Dr. Frank and the board of curators, the feeling was mutual that a parting of the ways was inevitable, resulting in Dr. Frank eventually submitting a letter of resignation. However, what preceded that action was ugly and unprofessional.

At the beginning of the board of curators meeting on a Saturday morning, Dr. Frank was abruptly informed by the board president that his services as president of Lincoln University were no longer needed; therefore, they were terminating his tenure as president of Lincoln University.

The board of curators had hired a person to do a written evaluation of Dr. Frank. The "one-man team" hired was a good friend of Otis Jackson, president of the board. Jackson and Frank disagreed on many issues, including the primary, fundamental role of the board. One of the numerous examples is the board making the decision, without consultation, collaboration, input, or evaluation from Dr. Frank, to eliminate the football team. Jackson said it was the board's prerogative to unilaterally disband the football program. That act alone was detrimental to the students and the University in so many ways. Numerous acts which took place were entirely out of line, blatant, and unprecedented.

Although the board members had paid for the services, they did not wait for the evaluation results which was probably never their intention in the first place. Instead, at a Saturday morning board meeting, the board President abruptly told Dr. Frank that his services were no longer needed, so he left the meeting. Dr. John Chavis, vice president, was told to assume the role of interim president. They later asked Dr. Frank to resign, and he refused to do so. Subsequently, Dr. Frank's attorney confirmed that the board of curators had acted illegally regarding the time frame, contractual agreements, and Missouri employment laws. Eventually, an agreement was reached between Dr. Frank and the board of curators. He remained on the payroll and continued to live in the president's house for several months, deciding to submit his resignation letter effective July 1, 1983, exactly ten years after he had become president. The night before that life-changing Saturday morning meeting, some board members had a secret meeting to plot their actions. At least two board members, who they knew would be in opposition to their planned actions and also alert Dr. Frank, were not informed about the meeting. Many of the board's actions were clearly and unbelievably not in accordance with the proper function of college boards.

When Dr. Frank returned home early that Saturday morning and told his wife what had happened, she was disappointed, but not completely surprised because of how actions had been unfolding. She conversed with him for a long time, giving support and encouragement, then braced herself for the unforeseen circumstances certain to be embedded in the days ahead.

Shortly after the day Dr. Frank resigned, every board member, who had been involved in the egregious attempt to micromanage, was declared ineligible to serve on the board and was summarily dismissed by the governor of Missouri from serving on the Lincoln University board of curators. That just gave credence to the existence of a malfunctioning Board of Curators. It gave Dr. Frank no sense of glee that the members were released but rather a sense of relief that a new board could now get back on track in adequately conducting the business of Lincoln University.

This was not how Dr. Frank had planned to conclude this chapter of his journey at Lincoln. At that time, he had no plans to leave Lincoln. However, Dr. Frank never looked back with regrets about how he interacted with the board. He was content with the stance he had taken in opposition to some of the Board members' uninformed preferences, many of which would have been detrimental to the University, and in opposition to board policy and common sense. Dr. Frank could proudly look back at the positions he had taken on issues. He had been guided by God, his moral compass, board policies, administrative insights, and acumen.

He felt deep in his soul that, for whatever reason, the script was in accordance with the universe, and affairs were unfolding the way they should. With that firm conviction in hand, he moved forward. He knew, through legal counsel, that he had more than sufficient grounds to file a lawsuit against the University, and his wife briefly thought that he should. Dr. Frank felt very strongly that it was time to leave, and rather than get involved in a legal battle, he would prefer to spend that time exploring new paths, and that is exactly what he did. It was not with joy that he left Lincoln and fond memories and unfinished projects and plans, but ironically, a sense of "It's Okay" prevailed and resonated deep within his soul. And, as fate would have it, the numerous friends and relatives who called to inquire about the situation, through their comments, unwittingly reinforced the same spirit.

The universe was indeed in agreement. Jesus said, "In the world, you have tribulation and trials, and distress and frustration; but be of good cheer (John 16:33 AMP)." And Dr. Frank, the visionary with inner calm and determination, marched on to the next chapter in what was yet to be an even more fruitful and exciting adventure. They meant it for evil, but God meant it for good.

When Dr. Frank submitted his letter of resignation in 1983, the members of the board of curators, based on information obtained from the Lincoln University archivist, Mr. Mark Schleer, were as follows:[29]

1. Otis Jackson, President
2. Geraldine Morris, vice president
3. Mildred Watson, secretary
4. Robert Chiles, treasurer
5. Paul Bloch
6. Craig Davis
7. Queenie Fowler
8. Michael Williams

---

[29] Obtained from Lincoln University Archivist, Mark Schleer, 2018

As of this writing, Dr. Frank is the only Lincoln University alumnus to become president of the University, having first returned to Lincoln University in 1956 as a professor and head basketball coach. In 2016, Lincoln celebrated its sesquicentennial Anniversary. The university has reportedly graduated more than 30,000 students during those years. Including Dr. Frank, only five alumni have become college presidents. They are Dr. Lionel Newsome (Central State University, Xenia, Ohio), Dr. Henry Givens (Harris Stowe University, St. Louis Missouri), Dr. John Smith (Fisk University, Nashville, Tennessee), and Dr. Albert Walker (Harris Stowe University, St. Louis, Missouri).

Drs. James & Zelma Frank at a University social function
during his successful tenure as president

The culmination of his tenure as president of Lincoln University and president of the NCAA marked the end of another season. The journey continued as the role of Southwestern Athletic Conference Commissioner began. In leaving the Lincoln University presidency, he could unquestionably look back on years well spent, some of the most productive in his life. The Lincoln University Alumni Oath reads, "We will never disgrace Lincoln University by any act of cowardice or dishonesty. We will fight for the ideals and sacred things of the University. We will transmit our university to those who come after us, greater, better, and more beautiful than it was transmitted to us." Dr. Frank left Lincoln University better than it was transmitted to him, as delineated in the Oath. He departed Lincoln with a legacy of firsts, integrity, great honor, and magnificent progress in moving the University forward. As an alumna, this writer says "Thank You."

Chapter 9

The Best of All Worlds – Commissioner, Southwestern Athletic Conference (SWAC)

1983 to 1998,
Interim, 2001 to 2003

Dr. Frank's impact and legacy with the NCAA and the Southwestern Athletic Conference are truly remarkable. He was a true pioneer in the field of collegiate athletics and his vision and legacy continue to positively impact countless student-athletes both past and present.

The Southwestern Athletic Conference will forever be indebted to Dr. Frank and his contributions to the SWAC. We will continue to strive daily to embody the core principles of his amazing leadership.
Charles McCleland,
SWAC Commissioner, 2018-Present

Keep in touch with the true needs in the lives of the people for whom you are responsible. walk in their shoes so that yours and theirs will be a better match.
James Frank

Dr. Frank is one of the few individuals who has risen through the collegiate ranks as a student-athlete, coach, educator, college president, and conference commissioner.
Dr. Myles Brandt,
Former NCAA President

Dr. Frank presiding at a Southwestern Athletic Conference dinner.

Shortly after he resigned from Lincoln, Dr. Frank received a phone call from a friend, Dr. Joseph Johnson, then president of Grambling State University in Grambling, Louisiana. He asked Dr. Frank if he would consider doing a research study on the Southwestern Athletic Conference (SWAC) and making recommendations on how it could be improved. The SWAC, established in 1920, is one of the many divisional athletic conferences of the NCAA. It is Division I for all sports. In football, the conference is a part of the NCAA's Football Championship Subdivision (FCS), formerly classified as "Division I-AA." Among other notable identifiers, it is one of the five Historically Black Colleges and Universities (HBCU) conferences. The other conferences are Mid-Eastern Athletic Conference (MEAC), Southern Intercollegiate Athletic Conference (SIAC), Central Intercollegiate Athletic Association (CIAA), and Gulf Coast Athletic Conference (GCAC). At that time, nine universities composed the SWAC, but the conference never had a full-time commissioner, staff, or home office. The member schools were Grambling State, Southern University, Prairie View, Alcorn, Arkansas State, Mississippi Valley, Jackson State, Texas Southern, and Alabama State. All SWAC schools are in the southern part of the United States.

Season of the SWAC

Dr. Frank accepted the offer to consult and was hired to do the research study. After the study was completed, he reported his findings to Dr. Johnson, who in turn reported them to the Council of Presidents (presidents of each of the SWAC schools). The council of presidents was so impressed with the study that they asked Dr. Frank if he would be willing to accept a full-time position as commissioner and initiate the recommendations he had outlined. After some deep reflection on many matters and characteristic consultation with his wife, he accepted the full-time position of SWAC Commissioner.

Pursuant to leaving Lincoln University, the decision to accept the position of SWAC commissioner rather than another college presidency seemed relatively easy and seemingly predestined. Athletics had been a part of his life for so long, and the prospect of working with over nine HBCUs was exciting and challenging. The move from college president to conference commissioner was comfortable. Mr. Lucius Jones, the husband of his administrative assistant, a good friend, and professor in the industrial arts department at Lincoln University told Dr. Frank that he would just love being SWAC commissioner because of the historic Bayou Classic, football weekends, and all of the excitement surrounding

SWAC sports activities. He was adamant in his declaration that "You are going to enjoy your new job." The Franks realized later on that Mr. Jones's words were prophetic - he was right that Dr. Frank would truly enjoy his new job!

Having done the analytical research study, Dr. Frank was thoroughly knowledgeable about what was needed. One of the changes Dr. Frank recommended in his study was that the conference office be located in the Superdome in New Orleans, Louisiana, because of its strategic location regarding the universities in the conference. The Council of Presidents was unanimous in its acceptance of the recommended location, so New Orleans, Louisiana would be where he set up the SWAC Commissioner's Office and where the Franks would make their new home. How exciting!

When the Franks moved to New Orleans, Dr. Frank's wife accepted a position as a reading consultant in an elementary school on the west bank. In 1984, after one year in that job, she was hired as director of student support services and an English professor at Southern University in New Orleans (SUNO). She held that position for twenty-three years.

Upon their arrival in New Orleans in 1983, Dr. Frank arranged to have the SWAC office located on the Southern University at New Orleans campus (SUNO) because the space in the Superdome was not ready for occupancy. The office on the campus was in the physical education building. The chancellor, Dr. Emmett Bashful, was very accommodating and welcomed the SWAC presence on campus. He assisted Dr. Frank in finding an administrative assistant and ensured the office was comfortable and strategically located. Dr. Frank sincerely appreciated Dr. Bashful's cooperative spirit and assistance.

SUNO is not a member of the SWAC because it is a commuter university and has no football team. However, Southern University in Baton Rouge, Louisiana, is a member of the SWAC. The Southern University system is composed of Southern University in New Orleans, Southern University in Baton Rouge, and Southern University in Shreveport. It is the only HBCU University system in the United States. Each campus has a chancellor, and the president oversees the operation of the three campuses.

The Louisiana Superdome

The SWAC office was located on the SUNO campus for approximately two months before Dr. Frank moved it to the Louisiana Superdome in New Orleans. Obtaining office space in the Superdome was not easily accomplished. Office space was minimal and not rented to athletic conferences. The Sugar Bowl occupied an office, but no other sports offices were there. Dr. Frank had negotiated with the decision-makers to obtain the office space that the SWAC was getting ready to occupy. The office was spacious, located on the main corridor, and near the popular Superdome restaurant where the gumbo was indescribably delicious! Also, Dr. Frank could step out of his office, sit in the stadium, and watch games. It was a super Superdome location.

The Superdome in New Orleans, currently named Caesar's Superdome is, more than just a sports complex. It is a domed stadium, one of the first of its kind, and serves many other purposes outside the realm of sports. It is in the Central Business District and is the home stadium for the NFL New Orleans Saints, The Sugar Bowl, the New Orleans Bowl, and the Bayou Classic. It has been the site of many sporting events, including Super Bowls and NCAA Final Four Championship games. The stadium has been in operation since August 3, 1975.

When Hurricane Katrina hit New Orleans on August 29, 2005, approximately 30,000 people sought refuge in the Superdome. Many had no means of leaving the city. Some died inside the stadium, and some outside. The mental and physical suffering inside the Dome was unbelievable. The wind and rain ripped holes in the roof of the Super Dome and did significant damage to the building and its temporary inhabitants. Toilets overflowed, people were hungry and hot and had no means to shower. The stench became unbearable. One of the viral images was an older deceased Black lady, covered with a blanket, sitting in a wheelchair in front of the Ernest N. "Dutch" Morial Convention Center. Compounding the sadness the picture provoked, the Convention Center was named after Dutch Morial, the first Black mayor of New Orleans, Louisiana.

To have occupied office space in the Superdome in 1983, before Hurricane Katrina, was prestigious. The location was ideal for conducting SWAC business. It was easily accessible, parking was sufficient, and the proximity to SWAC schools was convenient. The location of the colleges enhanced travel arrangements and communication within the Conference.

Another interesting tidbit is that Muhammad Ali defeated Leon Spinks at the Superdome on September 15, 1978, in a rematch for the World Boxing Association Heavyweight Championship, making him the first three-time world heavyweight champion. That was Ali's last professional boxing win.

The SWAC - Challenge and Change

Being the first full-time commissioner of the SWAC, overcoming the inertia and natural hindrances that beset a sixty-three-year-old HBCU athletic conference was a daunting challenge. Yet, as always, Dr. Frank met this challenge with the heart, mind, determination, and professionalism of a proven champion. Establishing the conference headquarters at the Superdome in New Orleans was a significant accomplishment but only the first step in bringing the conference into its most significant era of prominence.

Having been established in 1920, the Southwestern Athletic Conference (SWAC) had the history and potential to be considered the premier HBCU Conference and perhaps even more. For Dr. Frank, the transition from being a college president to becoming the commissioner of this conference was seemingly predestined. As a result of the research study he had recently completed, he was knowledgeable about the strengths and weaknesses of the conference; therefore, he was prepared to begin implementing a program to address the issues immediately.

One set of obvious issues Dr. Frank faced early in his tenure were challenges surrounding the Annual Bayou Classic football game during Thanksgiving weekends at the Superdome. The competition started in 1932 at Tulane University in New Orleans, Louisiana but was not given the name Bayou Classic until 1974. It is a game between the Southern University Jaguars and the Grambling State University Tigers and is played in New Orleans, Louisiana. The game is the highlight of the SWAC football season and a New Orleans tradition. It is one of the biggest football games during Thanksgiving weekend, including those within the larger football conferences. Thousands of people attend the game. For two years after Hurricane Katrina hit New Orleans, the game was played elsewhere, and attendance suffered during that period. Commissioner Frank was involved in ongoing negotiations regarding television network coverage of the Classic. The Bayou Classic has now been broadcast on NBC every Thanksgiving weekend since 1991. The broadcast created national attention and increased the fan base. The telecast includes showcasing the rich academic history and athletic traditions of the two schools, including features on famous alumni of the schools, and of course, the spectacular marching bands!

The primary issue was that the NCAA rules prevented schools in the then Division I- AA (now Football Championship Series) from competing at that late point in the season. Dr. Frank met with the executive committee of the NCAA and successfully persuaded the decision-makers to allow the continuance of the game. It would have been a significant loss and disappointment to the players and thousands of football fans had the NCAA not granted special permission for the game to continue. Grambling State was coached by the late, great coach Eddie Robinson for many years. He was college football's winningest coach for many of those years, retiring in 1997 as third on the all-time wins list with a record of 408-165-15. Thanks to Dr. Frank's strong and proactive leadership, the game continues.

Under Dr. Frank's leadership, consistency in the scheduling of events and positive publicity improved tremendously. The conference became more well-known, and its image and national recognition skyrocketed. It became highly recognized as a robust, respectable conference. During his tenure, Dr. Frank was highly respected by the other commissioners. Under his leadership, the conference rose to a higher level as he orchestrated many changes and improvements.

Dr. Frank at the Heritage Bowl which he founded with the Mid-Eastern Athletic Conference (MEAC) Commissioner Ken Free as the annual football game between the Championship teams of both conferences

Accomplishments

Some of his accomplishments follow:

1. Improved officiating and hired the first Supervisor of Officials for football and basketball;

2. Obtained sponsorships from Coke, McDonald's, and Reebok, and increased the number of other corporate sponsors;

3. Created the SWAC Football Championship Game;

4. Improved fundraising for the conference overall;

5. Increased the office staff, assigning specialists for specific areas of conference management and development;

6. Improved SWAC image, brought greater visibility, and elevated the conference to recognition and respect on the national stage;

7. Improved the relationship and lines of communication between the SWAC Commissioner and Athletics Directors;

8. Created a greater sense of unity and communication between all constituents in the SWAC;

9. Improved game scheduling;

10. Brought in two new schools: The University of Arkansas-Pine Bluff and Alabama A&M University – expanding the Conference to ten universities;

11. Approved the award named in his honor - the James Frank Commissioner's Cup - awarded annually to the school with the highest combined total of men's and women's all-sport points;

12. The creation of the original Freedom Bowl, which became the McDonald's Heritage Bowl, which has now morphed into the nationally televised SWAC - MEAC Challenge;

13. Improved the administration of The Bayou Classic;

14. Established the SWAC Hall of Fame in 1992, which has since inducted a distinguished group of former HBCU history makers such as Coach Eddie Robinson, Junious "Buck" Buchanan, Mel Blount, Lou Brock, David "Deacon" Jones, Willis Reed, Jerry Rice, Otis Taylor, Walter Peyton, Doug Williams, and Paul "Tank" Younger. Dr. Frank was inducted as well in 2006;

15. Established the Eddie Robinson Award;

16. Improved and increased the television contracts with networks such as BET, ESPN, and NBC;

17. Increased African American membership on NCAA Committees; and

18. Helped the Conference routinely have the highest football attendance averages in NCAA Division 1-AA.

There were some critics along the way, which is expected when changes have to be made. However, Dr. Frank addressed those problematic areas with courage, conviction, and a professional resolve that elevated the conference to historic levels.

SWAC Rewards

Dr. Frank became acquainted with the university presidents in the SWAC Conference and looked forward to meeting with them when he visited their campuses. His goal was to spend quality time with each one as often as time would permit. Interestingly enough, he and Dr. Joe Johnson, former president of Grambling State University, remained friends and kept in touch for the rest of their lives. They belonged to the same organization in Atlanta, Georgia, the HBCU Council of Past College Presidents. Dr. Frank played an essential role in other people's lives, as did others in his life - Dr. Joe Johnson was one of those persons.

As commissioner, he was a member of the College Commissioners Association (CCA). The organization was composed of all Division 1 college commissioners in the United States. The Association met annually in a different state each year, and the experiences were inspirational, informative, and challenging. He became acquainted with the other conference commissioners.

Drs. James and Zelma Frank with legendary comedian and activist Dick Gregory at the St. Louis Gateway Classic Football Foundation Coaches Luncheon in St. Louis, MO, 2002

During these times, the Commissioner's spouses also got to know each other well. Mrs. Frank enjoyed those interactions and developed some long-lasting friendships. With joy and excitement, she still recalls the many fun-filled activities scheduled for the Commissioners' wives during those conferences. They included luncheons, museums, shopping, sightseeing tours, water rafting, and other social gatherings. The Commissioners and their spouses usually got together for dinner every evening at an upscale restaurant. Those gatherings were always lively and fun-filled. At that time, Dr. Frank and Mr. Ken Free, commissioner of the Mid-Eastern Athletic Conference (MEAC), were the only Black Commissioners in the group, and the number is still minuscule. As of this writing, three African Americans have been hired and are either still serving or have served as NCAA Division I Commissioner. Those individuals are Keith Gill of the Sun Belt Conference, Kevin Warren of the Big Ten, and Andrea Williams, formerly of the Big Sky Conference, but now Chief Operating Officer of the NCAA Bowl Championship Series.

Yet, this job category (Collegiate Conference Commissioner) remains, to a certain degree, a "closed society" as far as opportunities for African Americans. They are generally limited to positions in HBCU conferences. There is a need for diversity and equal opportunity in the selection of College Commissioners for non-HBCU conferences.

The SWAC commissioner's job responsibilities included visiting the different Universities in SWAC. Therefore, Dr. Frank traveled throughout the South and witnessed the positive and negative aspects of life in the South. Sometimes, while riding along narrow country roads, he saw poor people living in shanties. These sights were disturbing and a reminder of how much more needs to be done for those in the United States who are disenfranchised. On the other hand, he recalls the beauty of the Southern terrain and the peaceful, long, music-filled drives to and from the Universities in the car with his wife and youngest son, Troy, who was a student at McDonough #35 Senior High School in New Orleans at the time.

Troy later graduated from Michigan State University with a BS in political science, the United States Sports Academy, with a master's degree in sports management, and earned his doctor's degree in business management from Webster University in St. Louis. He is now a professor at Lincoln University where his father's college career began.

Trent, Dr. Frank's elder son, missed out on a lot of those great football weekends at the SWAC HBCUs because he was on active duty as an officer in the United States Army. After graduating from Morehouse College, Trent married Pamela "Pam" Jones, joined the Army as a first lieutenant, and over twenty-one years later retired as a lieutenant colonel. He was ordained a Protestant minister in the interim and later received a Master of Divinity degree from Emory University. Fortunately, he and Pam were able to attend some of the SWAC games during Dr. Frank's tenure as commissioner.

During the SWAC years, the weekend trips usually included leaving home (New Orleans) on a Friday evening and returning home on Sunday afternoon. Each weekend, the Franks drove from New Orleans, Louisiana, to a different beautiful SWAC campus and enjoyed watching the football game and lively band. In addition to the weekend trips, Dr. Frank also enjoyed his role in the planning and staging of SWAC sporting events. Those were indeed moments to remember!

Mrs. Frank and Troy, having visited only a few HBCUs before that time, were amazed at the beauty and expanse of the campuses, the size of the student bodies, the quality of facilities, the electrifying excitement in the air, and, of course, the world-renowned marching bands! It was enlightening. Mrs. Frank felt a kinship with each university, having attended all-Black public schools in Kansas City, Missouri, and graduated from an HBCU (Lincoln University in Missouri). She felt that she was an alum of whichever college she was visiting at the time. Those weekends were filled with unimaginable joy and anticipation. Thank God for those moments!

In 1989, During Dr. Frank's sixth year as commissioner, the owners of a nationally known travel agency, FUGAZY, asked him if he would be interested in purchasing a franchise. The home office was located in Connecticut and held the contract for all NCAA travel. After considerable thought, reflection, and discussions with his wife, he decided to try his hand at entrepreneurship. He purchased a travel agency franchise and invited the mayor, Dutch Morial, the first Black mayor of New Orleans, to share in the purchase and partnership. Mayor Morial agreed to do so which launched another journey into unknown territory for Frank and his wife which would later include their oldest son and daughter-in-law.

They decided to locate the agency in downtown New Orleans. The name FUGAZY was emblazoned on the large, impressive entrance door. Some of the experiences involved new and different opportunities for travel, learning about the industry, paperwork, meetings, frequent oversight of the operations, and intricacies in hiring qualified personnel. Trent and his wife, Pam, moved to New Orleans, and both worked in managerial positions in the agency. Overall, it turned out to be an enjoyable, sometimes challenging experience for Dr. Frank and his family. Dr. Frank was now the creative off-sight manager in unchartered waters, and as usual, kept the ship firmly anchored and successfully on course steering it to its destination. Five years later, they decided the journey had been fulfilled and terminated the franchise.

Long after his tenure as SWAC Commissioner, Dr. Frank still liked to attend SWAC games. SWAC remained close to his heart, as evidenced by the SWAC paraphernalia that was still a regular part of his wardrobe long after retirement. He was asked what his most enjoyable job was and responded that being SWAC Commissioner was undoubtedly one of them. Dr. Frank thoroughly enjoyed being commissioner of the SWAC, but as the old saying goes, "all good things must come to an end." Finally, after a lifetime of service, Dr. Frank decided in 1996 to let the council of presidents know that he would be retiring two years later in 1998. Having been a college president, he knew that blindsided occurrences were unwelcome guests, so he decided to share that decision with the SWAC Council of Presidents far ahead of time. Although he was still enjoying his job, he felt it was time to retire and enjoy another lifestyle and the fruits of his lifelong endeavors.

When the time came for him to part ways with SWAC and retire as a lifelong educator and college sports leader, he had served as commissioner for fifteen years, and, after that, as interim commissioner for twenty months. His time as SWAC Commissioner afforded him the fantastic opportunity to remain actively involved in higher education and intercollegiate athletics, both of which he enjoyed.

He had always been very passionate about college athletics and community service. He set high standards for himself and those he was fortunate enough to lead. His many accomplishments, demeanor, philosophy, and desire to help and serve others garnered him many significant recognitions.

Chapter 10

Retirement – The Journey Continued

For me, becoming isn't about arriving somewhere or about achieving a certain aim. I see it instead as forward motion, a means of evolving, a way to reach continuously toward a better self. The journey doesn't end.
Michelle Obama

Don't count the days, let the days count.
Muhammad Ali

It's what you learn after you know it all that counts.
John Wooden

Dr. Frank behind the podium as Commissioner of the Southwestern Athletic Conference (SWAC)

The First and Second Retirement

The journey as SWAC Commissioner was an enjoyable one and Dr. Frank felt blessed to have had the opportunity to lead one of the nation's premier college conferences. He retired in 1998 with the full support and appreciation of the SWAC conference and its council of presidents. Dr. Frank's contributions to SWAC, college sports, and academic excellence nationwide over his entire career were remarkable.

The SWAC conference celebrated his retirement with much fanfare. His retirement recognition culminated in a beautiful retirement banquet at the Hotel Intercontinental in New Orleans. The one-time winningest college football coach, Eddie Robinson, delivered great words about the retiring commissioner, former college president, and former NCAA president. Robinson's wife presented roses to Zelma Frank on behalf of the conference and Dr. Frank who had requested that at the time of the presentation, he wanted a vocalist to sing, "You Are the Wind Beneath My Wings." Family, friends, and colleagues from far and near were present. Hundreds of people were in attendance.

Dr. Frank made a historical and moving farewell speech and received a standing ovation. Speakers delivered uplifting, memorable, historical, profound, and moving remarks and recognitions throughout the program, came from the speakers. The program epitomized "A Man for All Seasons," the program theme. This was a pivotal historical time in history. His youngest son, Troy, read the poem he had written for the occasion and received a standing ovation. It was a well-planned and dramatic retirement event, the memory of which lives on. Although unbeknownst to him, his retirement would be short-lived.

After he retired from SWAC, his successor as commissioner moved the Conference office to Birmingham, Alabama. Information about the new location was acknowledged with mixed reviews from parties closely associated with the conference. Shortly afterward, in 2000, the council of presidents decided to terminate the new commissioner's tenure. Dr. Frank was asked, urged, and finally persuaded by the president of the council of presidents to return to the SWAC as interim commissioner.

The decision was not an easy one for Dr. and Mrs. Frank. Dr. Frank had already settled into his retirement routine and was at perfect peace with his decision to have retired. Being interim commissioner would mean living in Birmingham during the week and flying home to New Orleans on weekends and back to Birmingham on Sunday evening or Monday morning. Just the thought of that schedule was unsettling. However, after much thought and deliberation, the Franks decided that, for the good of the conference, they would make the necessary sacrifices to enable Dr. Frank's return to the SWAC. Some weekends, Mrs. Frank flew to Birmingham to relieve Dr. Frank from constant weekly travel.

He held the position of Interim Commissioner for twenty months, developed meaningful relationships, and continued to move the conference forward in numerous ways. The conference office was located near the Civil Rights Institute. Basketball and football championships were held in Birmingham at the Birmingham Jefferson Convention Complex (BJCC) and Legion Field Stadium.

Dr. Frank and Norell established a scholarship for undergraduate student-athletes, in attendance at SWAC member institutions, during the time he served as interim commissioner. Dr. Norell, as mentioned earlier, was a professor and former athletics representative at Michigan State University. The scholarship was designed to encourage academic excellence and reward student-athletes who desired to pursue graduate studies in select fields.

This new season also included Dr. Frank becoming a grandfather. He visited his grandchildren as often as possible in Atlanta, Georgia, and was affectionately called "Papa." During this period, Trent and Pam, and the grandchildren would sometimes meet the Franks in Birmingham for basketball and football championship games.

Family Portrait (clockwise) Pam (Trent's wife), Trent (Son), Zelma, Troy (Son), Tracia (Granddaughter), Simeon (Grandson), and Dr. Frank

At the end of the twenty-month period as interim commissioner, Robert Vowels was hired. He picked up where Dr. Frank left off and expertly led the conference. Dr. Frank exited the post a second time amidst much praise and appreciation. As of this writing, the SWAC office is still located in Birmingham, Alabama.

That twenty-month span included the year 2001 when America experienced the attacks on the Twin Towers in New York and the Pentagon in the nation's capital. Dr. Frank was on an airplane flying from New Orleans to Birmingham on that fateful morning of 9/11. When the plane landed and the passengers deplaned, they were told, via a loudspeaker, about the terrorist attack on the United States. For safety concerns, they were momentarily detained at the airport.

Dr. Frank maintained contact and friendship with many of the individuals he supervised during his tenure as commissioner and interim commissioner, some of whom were as follows: Lonza Hardy, director, assistant commissioner for media relations, and later, associate commissioner, LaRita Greer Davenport, secretary, administrative assistant, and later, assistant commissioner for championships, Russell Stockard, publicity director, and later, director of compliance, Smita Parikh, business manager, Harold Clark, assistant publicity director, and later assistant media relations director, Dell Robinson, director of compliance, Jay Robertson, assistant commissioner, Nichelle Gainey, assistant commissioner of corporate partnership and marketing, George Evans, supervisor of Officials, Lawrence Collins, supervisor of officials, and Gilbert Stampley, attorney. He maintained contact with two commissioners who followed him, Robert Vowels, and Duer Sharp. The conference is currently headed by Dr. Charles McClelland whom Dr. Frank knew, contacted, and congratulated upon his appointment.

Dr. Frank's job, coupled with his wife's employment at Southern University in New Orleans as professor and director of student support services, kept them in New Orleans for 23 exciting and memorable years. However, those fantastic years included Hurricane Katrina. The Franks were living in New Orleans when Hurricane Katrina struck in 2005. Fortunately, he and his wife were out of the city on vacation at their summer home in Lake Ozark, Missouri. They watched the devastation on television with a very close friend, Cliff Flint, and Mrs. Frank's sister and brother-in-law, Mae and Cortez Bradley, who were vacationing with them. The Franks remained at their house in Lake Ozark for five months, making periodic trips back to New Orleans to assess the damage to their home.

Approximately six feet of water had flooded the home, and the entire first floor and its contents were destroyed. Lost items included photo albums, essential records, furniture, food, clothes, wedding pictures, and other irreplaceable items, along with a home that held beautiful memories. It is often forgotten that two weeks after Katrina, Hurricane Wilma swept through New Orleans. Wilma blew the chimney off of the house, shattered glass and scattered debris, leaving the second floor of the house in tatters. After Wilma, the only part of the home left intact was the attic. The Franks knew the only option was forward movement. Mrs. Frank had not retired, so they moved back to New Orleans in January 2006. Mrs. Frank resumed her duties at SUNO until she retired in 2007.

In 2006, Pam, the Frank's daughter-in-law, learned that she had a life-threatening illness, and in 2007, she transitioned from this life. The loss of their daughter-in-law prompted yet another significant move for the Franks, this time to Atlanta, Georgia, to be closer to their Grandchildren and be present with their son, Trent, in raising them. They made that move in the spring of 2008.

Atlanta provided another opportunity for Dr. Frank to continue his contribution to education and his service to HBCUs. He was able to join with other retired former HBCU presidents on the HBCU Council of Former Presidents. These men and women offered their expertise, guidance, and assistance to current HBCU presidents. The group met monthly in a building at the Atlanta University Center where the following colleges are located: Clark Atlanta University, Morehouse College, Spelman College, Morris Brown College, and the Interdenominational Theological Seminary (ITC). When he went to meetings at the Atlanta University Center, he was reminded of the time, many years earlier, when he was hired by Clark, Atlanta University as a consultant to evaluate their entire athletics department and sports program.

Atlanta's proximity to Birmingham allowed the Franks, son Trent, and two grandchildren, Tracia, and Simeon, to spend some beautiful weekends in Birmingham attending SWAC championship games and visiting the Civil Rights Museum and other historic locations.

Retirement is not an easy transition for some people. However, Dr. Frank, beginning with his first retirement, moved into that new lifestyle with the same grace, dignity, optimism, and confidence displayed throughout his career. To him, it was simply an option that he had chosen. He never second-guessed himself about having made that decision although he had thoroughly enjoyed every step along the way of his long, meaningful, and illustrious journey. It was just time to turn another corner.

Always Making a Difference

Dr. Frank continued his involvement with SWAC and Lincoln University. He maintained the scholarships in his name at both SWAC and Lincoln. His wife continues to monitor those scholarships.

As it pertained to Lincoln, he felt indebted to the school that had done so much for him. He continued to give of his time, talent, and monetary resources, well into his retirement. In addition to staying engaged with the local Atlanta Lincoln University Alumni Chapter, he made contributions to the university that were varied and significant. Some instances follow.

When he received the Gerald R. Ford Award in 2008, he donated the $25,000.00 award to the Lincoln University Athletic Department. The award was matched by Title 11 Funds. Additionally, he was also one of the original planners who founded the Lincoln University Athletics Hall of Fame, also in 2008. Because of his momentous contributions to the NCAA, the organization set up a $10.000.00 endowed scholarship in his name at Lincoln University.

Despite the time and energy required for his activities on the national stage, Dr. Frank continued to serve the University through the Lincoln University Foundation, becoming a leader in fundraising. For instance, When Lincoln tore down Memorial Hall and built a new one, Dr. Frank drove the fundraising for that project. He also helped raise money for the newest building on campus, the Linc Recreation and Wellness Center, by contacting friends for donations. He raised over $69,000.00 through his letter-writing campaign. The north wing of this building was named after him in 2017.

The Linc Recreation & Wellness Center

He initiated and carried out the drive to pay off the $750,000 debt for the $2 million Soldier's Memorial Plaza. As a part of the funds raised, Dr. Frank was able to raise a $50,000 donation from his class of 1953. A plaque that bears his name and the names of his classmates is on the campus in honor of that successful endeavor.

Dynamic bronze statues are the highlight of the Soldier's Memorial Plaza at the center of the Lincoln University campus. The inscription reads "Dedicated to the officers and soldiers of the 62nd and 65th Regiments of the United States Colored Infantries."

He continued to make annual financial contributions to Lincoln University in many areas. Over the course of his distinguished life, Dr. Frank contributed over $300,000 to Lincoln in personal gifts. His generosity, fundraising and various scholarships will continue to have an indelible impact on Lincoln's current and future students.

Dr. Frank accepted speaking engagements and continued to attend relevant conferences, workshops, and seminars, and Lincoln University Homecomings. He knew how important it was to stay physically and mentally fit, so he was motivated to continue his routine trips to the YMCA or one of the nearby fitness facilities and play golf on a regular basis. He spent a lot of time with friends, associates, and family, particularly his two grandchildren. During retirement, he often reflected on many different aspects of his life.

He fully appreciated that life is made up of memorable moments. The most precious of those moments is always NOW!

Dr. Frank with longtime Lincoln University Archivist, Mark Schleer, at the Homecoming football game in 2014. (Photograph by Marguerite Schleer)

Dr. James Frank, Ms. Nichelle Gainey, former Assistant Commissioner of Corporate Partnership and Marketing at SWAC, and Mrs. Frank at the 2015 NCAA Final Four "Meet and Greet Dr. James Frank" event in Indianapolis, Indiana. (Photograph from Frank family collection)

Dr. James Frank and nephew Clifton Johnson at the 2015 NCAA Final Four "Meet and Greet Dr. James Frank" that Clifton organized in Indianapolis, Indiana

Dr. James Frank and Family at a 2015 NCAA Final Four "Meet & Greet Dr. James Frank" in Indianapolis, Indiana

Chapter 11

A Man for All Seasons

A man who is successful and talented in many areas. a man who is ready to cope with any contingency and whose behavior is always appropriate to every occasion.
Idioms by The Free Dictionary

Aspire to do right by the others in your family, on your team, and in your community, and you lay the foundation, not just for successful endeavors, but for the successful relationships upon which any good life must rely.
James Frank

During a long and distinguished career of over 50 years, Frank's efforts and influential leadership touched the lives of countless people and resulted in positive changes in the many organizations he served.
HBCU Buzz.com

Dr. Frank is one of the few individuals who has risen through the collegiate ranks as a student-athlete, coach, educator, college president, and Conference Commissioner.
Myles Brand, Former President, NCAA

THE SOUTHWESTERN ATHLETIC CONFERENCE
Salutes

DR. JAMES FRANK
"A Man for All Seasons"

Thursday, May 21, 1998   The Hotel Inter-Continental   New Orleans, Louisiana

*Cover of the Retirement Program from the Southwestern Athletic Conference
(SWAC), Thursday, May 21, 1998, at the Hotel Inter-Continental,
New Orleans, LA*

Dr. Frank was once asked, "What advice would you give to young people today who want to be successful, whether or not in leadership roles?" His response was, "Work hard, be honest and fair in your dealings with people, and adopt the Boy Scout motto, "Be Prepared." In the final analysis, those principles describe the way he lived his own life which resulted in his enormous success.

Because of the depth and scope of Dr. Frank's career, he had to function in many different roles; therefore, earning the title, "A Man for All Seasons." This journey started with his birth on October 6, 1930, in a small steel mill town, Aliquippa, Pennsylvania, located north of Pittsburgh, and led to historic achievements at the national level.

He traveled from high school star basketball player to college star basketball player, college professor, basketball coach, dean of students, vice president, only alumnus to become president of his alma mater, secretary-treasurer, and first African American president of the NCAA, and first full-time Southwestern Athletic Conference Commissioner (SWAC). Interspersed with all of the grandeur and busyness, he was immersed in the roles of husband, father, uncle, grandfather, brother, friend, mentor, and counselor.

Dr. Frank, "A Man for All Seasons," is understandably the best description of him and was the theme for his retirement celebration. That sentiment is reflected in the poem written by his younger son, Troy. He wrote it specifically for his father's retirement. It is accurate, poetically profound, and reflective of his interpretation of his father's life. Troy received a standing ovation when he read the poem at Dr. Frank's SWAC Retirement celebration on Thursday, May 12, 1998, at the Hotel Intercontinental in New Orleans, Louisiana.

Jim, A Man for All Seasons

By Troy Frank

Young man, from the Pennsylvania Hills;
Barely shoes,
Barely clothes,
Barely food,
Barely a bed to shield this child from winter's bitter chill.

Five brothers, two sisters,
and a mother he barely knew--
She died,
Yet youth did not grant him time to rue,
For it was then that he learned that life was as unpredictable as it
could be cruel.

Yet,

The Father was still there…   Proprietor,
Taskmaster,
Stern Hand,
And in the end, Preacher.

He, in his way, like the ice trucks after school,
Basketball in December
Baseball over the Allegheny in June,
And the soot and grime of the steel mills were now his life's
preeminent teachers.

Aliquippa… a genuinely American slice of pie,
baked and seasoned by the riches of our nation's steel,
Demure, and proud in its stature,
Pride,
Hope,
and honesty are the sons
birthed from its legacy that composes its nomenclature.

In this town, he played the games boys play.
With the wood and rawhide serving as the tools of the trade that
marked each day.

These skills gleaned from the Keystone State's soil,
Would precipitate his life's rewards through this youthful
and disciplined toil.

Then, he journeyed to the Great Midwest; 'Po boy from
Pennsylvania on a train, to a strange
land where no one knew his name…

Lincoln University!
Named for the Great Emancipator,
and Mecca for our nation's young and colored best.

It was here that he would learn, write, teach, coach, read, and
ultimately lead,
And the memories of the bitter sacrifices of his youth would be
laid to rest.

The Student: A dedicated scholar driven by the discipline derived
from his youth,

The Teacher: A molder of young minds made erudite by the
maintenance and maturity melded from the smell of molten metal
from the steel mills back home that told him he wanted a different
life.

The Athlete: A gamesman with an aura and confidence bearing
gifts that were a Godsend on which his teammates could always
depend,
And, President: Salient spokesperson for the Black College cause;
Negotiator, fund-raiser, and warrior for the righting of historical
wrongs;

A visionary,
An architect of an institutional destiny and molder
of the minds of all its gifted progeny.

Then, he was called to Korea – one of those faraway places that he
had only read about in books that he took from shelves… It was
here that the seeds were sown, harboring monumental challenges
for him he had never imagined or known.

An American soldier called to engineer in a faraway land,
Building bridges and helping little children while upholding his
military
duty to protect, serve, and defend,

Only to return to the Great Midwest to capture a freckle-faced
redhead from Kansas City who
became his lifelong partner and best friend.

Through a life lived, and many battles fought, through friends
made, and the comfort of opinion constantly sacrificed in favor of
the rigors of thought,

Some came to know him as the first 'Brotha in the pulpit at the
NCAA convention—

A cool customer and poised diplomat balancing the pendulum of
agreement and dissension.
Some came to know him as the director of an epic saga, the first
College President to run this most August of all shows – executing
every instruction in times of both elation and frustration, keeping a
varied cast of characters in tow.

Some know him as the Commissioner – Actor on a grand stage,
A meticulous author editing every detail on every page,
A keen facilitator and cunning administrator,
A spokesperson for our sporting culture and cadence,
A dedicated committee man serving as a granite pillar amidst
swirling trade winds using words and logic as the tools by which
he has taken his many stands.
The days of a lifetime,
Seasoned with accomplishment and shaped by the winds of time;
For the clock still chimes, for this is but the genesis of another
verse of life's song full of syncopation and rhyme.

For one need only look at your posture, face, and gait to see that
Father Time has indeed been kind,
As he will continue to sweeten the glow of your
legacy through the ages,
like wine.

For this has been his life's story,
His Hard Road to Glory,
Latin oration would tell us Carpe' Diem! – meaning Seize the day!
Yes, you have seized the day and done it your way,
Like the old Sinatra tune, That's Life tells us,
You have ridden high in your Aprils and been shot down in your
Mays,
But you arose again like the Fiery Phoenix to live to fight and
conquer yet another day.

Mr. B would sing to you that The Prime of Your Life had begun at
last tonight, and the world is just one day old, and despite your
legacy and achievement, there is still work to be done and stories
yet to be told!

Lennon and McCartney would sing that tonight is your yesterday,
and all of your troubles are indeed far away,

And with each new day and first glance at the sun, you have only
just begun.

This is a life of Shakespearean proportion;
from meek beginnings to achieve that which was inconceivable,
That which was unbelievable,

To stand here this fortnight to celebrate and pay tribute in part,
to this incredible journey that can be looked upon in whole, can
best be described as
a complex tapestry and brilliant work of art:

The Athlete
The Educator,
The Leader
The Teacher
The Coach,
The Commissioner,
The Trailblazer,
The President,
The Role Model,

Scholar, Father, and Friend,

Whether one has known him as Coach, Dr. Frank, Mr. President,
Jim, Jimmy, or
James, this is the legacy, and these are the reasons why he is truly
A Man for All Seasons.

Dr. Frank speaks at the 2008 NCAA National Convention after receiving the NCAA President's Gerald R. Ford Award. This annual award is the NCAA's top award and honors an individual who has provided significant leadership as an advocate for intercollegiate athletics continuously throughout their career.

Chapter 12

Awards, Honors, and Tributes

*Honor is a character quality that one should seek to have.
Honor is also the recognition given to one for possessing
that character quality.*
Trent Frank

*Some accolades are earned, and some are given. Dr.
Frank earned every accolade he received*
Zelma Frank

Humility and Honor Usually Walk Hand-in-Hand.
James Frank

*Dr. James Frank in his home office in 2014, seen with the Mahogany encased
Gerald R. Ford Award in the background*

Dr. Frank's awards, honors, and tributes have been numerous. In addition, he has achieved many "firsts," which makes him a trailblazer. He was asked by friends, more than once, where in his house could he find room to put another plaque or artifact representing an honor. Despite the thorough research done by the writer, some accolades were no doubt missed. She has made a sincere attempt, in this chapter, to paint an accurate picture of this great man and all his influence, as seen through the lens of awards, honors, and tributes.

The items listed in this chapter have been categorized by Awards as identified by tangible recognitions given to Dr. Frank and carry the title "Award." The Honors listed are the many other recognitions and acknowledgments of his extraordinary achievements. Finally, the tributes section contains only a few of the many written expressions of respect and admiration for Dr. Frank.

One of Dr. Frank's hometown honors was his selection as One of the Top 50 Greatest Sports Figures from The Valley. The Valley is the area of Pennsylvania that includes Aliquippa, Pennsylvania, Dr. Frank's birthplace. He was ranked #17. The criteria for selection speak volumes about everything Dr. Frank represented.

Awards

Dr. Frank has been inducted into ten halls of fame. Additionally, he has received many other honors and awards.

National Awards

❖ The annual NCAA President's Gerald R. Ford Award, named for the late United States president is the NCAA's top award which honors an individual who has provided significant leadership as an advocate for intercollegiate athletics continuously throughout his or her career, January 12, 2008

❖ James Corbett Award, the highest award given 0f the National Association of College Directors of Athletics (NACDA), awarded annually for devotion to the betterment of intercollegiate athletics, June 15, 1998

❖ All-American Football Foundation Outstanding College President's Award for outstanding performance in a chosen profession, 1998

❖ The National Football Foundation and College Hall of Fame, Inc. "Distinguished American Award," 2001 (Other recipients have been: Vince Lombardi, Pete Roselle, Sonny Werblin, Moose Krause, Joe Paterno, Tom Osborne, Rev. Edmund P. Joyce, and Roy Kramer.)

❖ Silver Anniversary Award for Commitment to Sports and Fitness, presented by The President's Council for Physical Fitness and Sports Dedication, September 9, 1981

Dr. Frank is Presented the National Black College Alumni
Hall of Fame Award in 1994 by Dr. Wendell Rayburn, President
of Lincoln University from 1988 to 1996

Other Awards

❖ First Black and the first college president to serve as NCAA President. Award presented at the thirty-sixth Annual Central Intercollegiate Athletic Association Basketball Tournament in Norfolk, Virginia, February 26, 1981

❖ On December 18, 2007, he was inducted into the Legends Class of Minority Athletic Administrators. At the inaugural event, Dr. Frank and five other African American trailblazers in athletic administration were honored. The other honorees were Wayne Embry, the first African American NBA General Manager; Ozzie Newsome, the first African NFL General Manager; Gene Smith, the first African American NACDA president; Dr. LeRoy Walker, first African American President of the NAIA and USOC; and Bill White, first African American Major League, and National League president.

❖ Wilson Hole In One Award – The Best of All Shots in the Golfing World, August 7, 1981

❖ Alumni Achievement Award in recognition as the only alumnus to be named president of Lincoln University, presented by the Greater St. Louis Alumni Chapter, July 15, 1983

❖ Pioneer Award for Contributions to Sports and Equal Opportunity for the Dignity of All Men, presented by The 100% Wrong Club, 1983

❖ Atlanta Life Insurance Company, Herndon Pioneer Award for outstanding contributions in sports, February 18, 1984

❖ Commitment and Service as SWAC Commissioner, Visionary Leadership Award for McDonald's Heritage Bowl, December 27, 1997

❖ Springfield College Distinguished Alumni Award, 2003

❖ Lifetime Achievement Award from St. Louis Gateway Classic Foundation

❖ Lifetime Achievement Award from SWAC Alumni Association, December 4, 2015, in Houston, Texas

❖ Lincoln University Foundation President's Leadership Award for leadership, philanthropy, and dedicated service, October 11, 2007

❖ Dick Gregory/Elston Howard Distinguished Sports Achievement Award presented by the Gateway Classic Sports Foundation and St. Louis Rams, 2007

❖ Aaron Elijah Lovejoy Award in recognition of outstanding accomplishments and leadership in academics and intercollegiate sports. presented by the Black Chamber of Commerce – Orange County, Los Angeles, California, 2008

❖ Lincoln University Fourth Annual Golf Tournament, All Greek Best Score Award, sponsored by the Divine Nine, 2014

❖ Pioneer Trailblazer Award, presented by Duplichain University, June 2, 2014

❖ Standing Ovation Award for a Legacy of Excellence, presented by the Lincoln University Class of 1964 on the occasion of their fiftieth Anniversary Celebration, October 18, 2014

❖ Legacy Tribute Award, presented by the Atlanta Lincoln University Alumni Chapter, March 2, 2019

❖ Lincoln University Trailblazer Award for Commitment to Education and Community

❖ The Because You Cared Award - Lincoln University Class of 1963 at fiftieth Anniversary Reunion

❖ College Commissioner's Association (CCA) Golf Tournament First Place Award for Low Gross (2001)

❖ Aliquippa Legends Award

❖ Listed as one of the Springfield College Notable Alumni

❖ Lincoln University, fourth Annual Golf Tournament, All Greek Best Score Award, 2014

Dr. Troy Frank, Dr. James Frank, Dr. Zelma Frank, Retired Lieutenant colonel, Trent Frank, during the Picture Unveiling in the Dr. James Frank Room at the NCAA National Headquarters, Indianapolis, IN

Honors

Honorary Degrees

❖ Honorary Doctorate Degree, Lincoln University, Jefferson City, Missouri, May 1983

❖ Honorary Doctorate Degree, Springfield College, Springfield, Massachusetts, May 17, 2009

Halls of Fame

❖ Inducted into the SWAC Hall of Fame, December 15, 2006

❖ Inducted into the 2016 Inaugural Class of the U. S. Army ROTC National Hall of Fame on June 10, 2016, at Fort Knox, Kentucky.

❖ Inducted into the Lincoln University Athletic Hall of Fame, 2009

❖ Inducted into the Lincoln University Alumni Hall of Fame, 2009

❖ Inducted into the Lincoln University ROTC Hall of Fame, 1975

❖ The National Black College Alumni Hall of Fame Foundation, 1994

❖ The Greater New Orleans Sports Hall of Fame, 1998

❖ The Beaver County Sports Hall of Fame, 1982

❖ Aliquippa High School Sports Hall of Fame, 1976

❖ Aliquippa Sports Hall of Fame, 1976

Additional Honors & Recognitions

❖ Southwestern Athletic Conference (SWAC) annual James Frank Commissioner's Cup Award is determined by team finish in respective sports

❖ Listed as a "Presidential First" in the Top 25 Defining Moments in NCAA History

❖ Listed by ESPN published him as among those on the NCAA's 100 Most Influential Student Athletes during the NCAA Centennial Celebration

❖ Inducted into the Inaugural 2007 Class of Minority Athletic Administrators

❖ Major conference room named in his honor containing his history and a commissioned portrait at the NCAA National Headquarters in Indianapolis, Indiana

❖ Listed in "Diversity Pioneers and Trailblazers," along with other notables including Condoleezza Rice, Senator Cory Booker, and Dr. Clifton Wharton, Diverse Magazine, January 14, 2016

❖ Featured during Black History Month, February 2016, The Times. (Beaver County in Pennsylvania)

❖ Listed in The Times newspaper of Beaver County, Sunday, April 24, 2016, as One of the Top 50 Greatest Sports Figures from The Valley.

❖ Lincoln University Alumni - Atlanta Chapter golf tournament named the Annual Dr. James Frank Tournament

❖ Springfield College Notable Alumni Roster along with individuals like James Naismith who invented the game of basketball

❖ Featured on a concrete wall that was specifically designed and built to honor Aliquippa area legends. The wall is labeled "Legends Plaza" and is in the Tony Dorsett Stadium in Hopewell Township (PA) 2012

❖ Appointed by United States President, Gerald Ford, to serve on the Board of Visitors at the United States Naval Academy to evaluate the athletic programs at the three service academies – Army, Navy, and Air Force

❖ One wing of the recently built LINC wellness center was named the Dr. James Frank Center, Lincoln University, September 22, 2017. Judge Marvin Teer, Jr., an alumnus and President of the Board of Curators at that time, said, "It is an honor well deserved. He was a guiding light for all of us."

The Dr. James Frank Center at the LINC, Lincoln University
Jefferson City, Missouri

❖ September 9, 2022, the Lincoln University Board of Curators, under the leadership of Board President, Victor B. Pasley, and in agreement with Lincoln University President, Dr. John Moseley, voted to rename Founders Hall, the Dr. James Frank Hall. Board of Curators: Vernon V. Bracy, Stacia Bradley Brown, Everidge Cade Jr., Richard G. Callahan, Richard R. Popp, Terry Rackers, Tina Shannon.

Tributes

From Former alumni

Whether he was at a sporting event, the barbershop, a supermarket, or just walking down the street, students would invariably approach him and make comments like the following:

I was a student when you were president of Lincoln University, and I always admired you;

You were my coach when I played basketball, and I remember all of the principles you taught us to live by; you were always my role model;

Because of what you taught me, I am where I am today;

I know you don't remember me, but you were *MY* president, you were my teacher, and I will always remember you.

You inspired me to get my Ph.D. because I wanted to be like you.

He has also received many positive comments and correspondences from former colleagues, friends, and acquaintances down through the years. The following submissions are representative of only a few.

Other Written and Oral Expressions

The following letter was sent to Dr. Frank when he was President of the NCAA, as noted on the letterhead.

The National Collegiate Athletic Association

President
JAMES FRANK
Lincoln University
Jefferson City, Missouri 65101

Executive Director
WALTER BYERS

Secretary-Treasurer
JOHN L. TONER
University of Connecticut
Storrs, Connecticut 06268

1981 COUNCIL

PRESIDENT
SECRETARY-TREASURER
DISTRICT VICE-PRESIDENTS
District One
ANDREW T. MOORADIAN
University of New Hampshire
District Two
OLAV B. KOLLEVOLL
Lafayette College
District Three
JOHN W. SAWYER
Wake Forest University
District Four
RICHARD G. SHRIDER
Miami University (Ohio)
District Five
ALDO A. SEBBEN
Southwest Missouri State University
District Six
CHARLES H. SAMSON
Texas A&M University
District Seven
JOSEPH R. GERAUD
University of Wyoming
District Eight
JOHN B. DAVIS
Oregon State University

VICE-PRESIDENTS-AT-LARGE
FRANCIS W. BONNER
Furman University
HOWARD DAVIS
Tuskegee Institute
CHALMER G. HIXSON
Wayne State University
JUDITH R. HOLLAND
University of California, Los Angeles
ELIZABETH A. KRUCZEK
Fitchburg State College
EDWIN W. LAWRENCE
Cheyney State College
EDWARD W. MALAN
Pomona-Pitzer Colleges
EDWIN D. MUTO
State University of New York, Buffalo
GWENDOLYN NORRELL
Michigan State University
DONALD M. RUSSELL
Wesleyan University
P. LAVERNE SWEAT
Hampton Institute
KENNETH J. WELLER
Central College (Iowa)

•

1981 EXECUTIVE COMMITTEE

PRESIDENT
SECRETARY-TREASURER
ERNEST C. CASALE
Temple University
LINDA K. ESTES
University of New Mexico
J. WILLIAM GRICE
Case Western Reserve University
ROBERT C. JAMES
Atlantic Coast Conference
HENRY T. LOWE
University of Missouri, Columbia
SEAVER PETERS
Dartmouth College
ROBERT F. RIEDEL
State University College, Geneseo
CHARLEY SCOTT
University of Alabama
JOE L. SINGLETON
University of California, Davis
MARY ZIMMERMAN
University of South Dakota

December 17, 1981

Mr. James Frank
President
Lincoln University
Jefferson City, Missouri 65101

Dear Jim:

Enclosed is a copy of an interesting article about you which recently was published in the Denver Post.

I enjoyed reading the article and appreciate very much the leadership you have provided in dealing with difficult issues such as restructuring.

Best wishes for the holiday season.

Sincerely,

Bill

William B. Hunt
Assistant Executive Director

WBH:koc
Enclosure

National Office: Nall Avenue at 63rd Street • Mission, Kansas
Mailing Address: P.O. Box 1906 • Shawnee Mission, Kansas 66222 • Telephone 913/384-3220

When Dr. Frank received the Gerald R. Ford Award, Myles Brandt, president of the NCAA at that time, said, "Dr. Frank is one of few individuals who has risen through the collegiate ranks as a student-athlete, coach, educator, college president, and Conference commissioner."

The following Correspondence of April 25, 2015 was from Joe Crowley, someone with whom Dr. Frank worked very closely during his time with the NCAA, a noted figure in the world of sports, and author of a book on the history of the NCAA, *In The Arena: The NCAA's First Century*, **and former President of the NCAA.**

Dear Jim, Ced Dempsey told me about the dedication of a room in your honor at the NCAA headquarters....I asked Ced to get me your email address so I could congratulate you on this overdue recognition. You have meant so much to the Association, in so many capacities, over the years – as the first university president to serve as NCAA president, the successful effort you led to bring women's sports into the organization when you were Secretary-Treasurer, the many challenges you dealt with (again, successfully) during those leadership years, your contributions to intercollegiate athletics as a player, conference commissioner and institutional president, and in so many other ways. It has been a privilege to know and learn from you, and especially to have the honor of being your friend. I wish I could have been there in April when the room was dedicated. Congratulations and best wishes.

Joe Crowley

NOTE: The celebration to which Crowley referred was for the unveiling of Dr. Frank's picture in the room that had already been dedicated many years earlier.

Excerpts from an email written by former colleague and friend, Dr. Bernard Gutin, with whom he worked while employed at Lehman College in the Bronx, New York, November 25, 2016

Our daughter, Linda, was here yesterday (Thanksgiving) and asked me to tell her about the fact that you were the first Black president of the NCAA. Of Course, I told her what I knew and said that we had talked over the phone a few months ago.

Regarding an interview online that Linda had shared with him, he wrote the following:

I viewed the interview and wanted to let you know how proud I am of having been your colleague and friend. The interviewer kept giving you chances to extol your accomplishments, but she could not get you to brag about anything more than your work ethic. It reminded me of how impressed I was when you were appointed chairman of some +committee or other at Hunter College. I don't think I took participation on committees very seriously (Please forgive me, I was only a rookie!) until you convened the first meeting and showed us how to do it. This was consistent with what you told the audience in the video: set reasonable goals and do the work necessary to achieve those goals. I suspect this humble attitude and work ethic was what accounted for your success in so many ventures.

Gutin, May 5, 2018;

Hi Jim, in our men's group meeting to be held today, we are supposed to talk about our favorite person (other than family, of course). I first thought about Jack Begelman, but I have already told the group about him as my favorite mentor. So, I went on to think about other favorite people: students who went on to be college presidents, teaching colleagues, dance teachers, etc. In this process, I realized that the main criterion I was using was the degree to which they contributed to the welfare of humanity, and I decided that Dr. James Frank was my favorite. So, I will be talking about this exemplary person in an hour or so. Of course, it goes without saying that I will be talking about Dr. Zelma Frank as well. If you feel your ears burning, that will be why.

Love from all the Gutins

And then there was the call from his high school classmate and lifelong friend, Michael Zernich, MD. (Deceased). He called unexpectedly one day to say hello and simply thank Dr. Frank for just being his friend over the years.

During a lunch break when Dr. Frank served on the Lincoln University Foundation Board, the writer was conversing with Professor Emeritus, Dr. Joe Simmons, a board member. Having served in numerous capacities under Dr. Frank when he was president of Lincoln University, he was recalling some of his fondest memories.

As of this writing, Dr. Simmons still serves on the Lincoln University Foundation Board. The writer asked him if he would put those memories in writing to be included in a book she was writing about Dr. Frank. He said he would. He later sent me a copy of his recollections which have been included here.

Correspondence by Dr. Joe L. Simmons

I had the distinct pleasure of working with Dr. James Frank while he served as the fourteenth president of Lincoln University of Missouri. Among his many attributes, I would like to point out some that truly spoke to who he truly was.

1. Dr. Frank was a great leader while he served as the president of Lincoln University.

2. He was a very good role model and always looked for the good in everyone.

3. Not only did he look for the good in individuals, but he would also assist in making it possible for those around him to reach their highest potential.

4. There were those of us who could not financially afford to pursue terminal degrees in our field of expertise. His favorite

saying was, "If you want to get ahead, you must continue your education until you earn the highest degree possible in your field. Then he would say, "You get in school, I will take care of the rest. Not only did he say it, but he also did it. I am one of those who could not afford to continue my education at the University of Missouri in Columbia, Missouri. He said to me, "Let me take care of that."

5. Dr. Frank would never accept anything but the best from those who worked in his administration.

6. Dr. Frank did not hesitate in making decisions. After hearing all of the facts in an unresolved controversial situation, he would say to you, "This must cease and desist. We have to move on with educating the students. I want this taken care of today. End of discussion!"

7. When Dr. Frank was no longer the president of Lincoln University, he and his lovely wife, Dr. Zelma Frank, never stopped supporting their alma mater. Today there are scholarships in the Lincoln University Foundation in their honor. They are still supporting students who want to continue their education and become productive citizens.

8. Dr. Frank served on the Lincoln University Foundation Board for many years. Because of his many accomplishments, and his ardent support of the University, Lincoln named a portion of the current LINC building, DR. JAMES FRANK CENTER. What an honor! It could not have happened to a better person.

9. While serving on the Lincoln University Foundation Board, Dr. Frank continued to offer suggestions for fundraising that would be in the best interest of the University. He would methodically lay out a complete plan and challenge the other board members to follow his lead to strengthen the institution.

10. Dr. Frank was never without words, and he never stopped trying to help people.

11. He has a wonderful legacy, and I am very proud to have had the opportunity to work and study under his tutelage.

Two other professors, emeriti, Dr. Nathan Cook, and Dr. Arnold Parks, have always held Dr. Frank in high esteem. This is evidenced in the context of a thorough letter they wrote to the university president in 2015 requesting that the administration rename Founders Hall in honor of Dr. Frank. They described him as "an alumnus who has demonstrated a commitment in many capacities and ways, to the advancement of Lincoln University for fifty-nine years. Additionally, he is a person who has achieved national acclaim and has brought national recognition to his alma mater. We see it as appropriate and fitting to pay homage to an individual who has given back his time and service to the institution which we all love." On September 9, 2022, seven years later, their request was realized when the board of curators voted to rename Founders Hall, the Dr. James Frank Hall.

Lincoln professors emeriti Dr. Arnold Parks, and Dr. Nate Cook with Dr. Zelma Frank and Dr. James Frank at Lincoln University during the naming of the Dr. James Frank Center on campus.

The influence and lessons learned from his father make up the content of the book his son, Trent, is writing about his father's leadership, "A Legacy of Moral Leadership: The Leadership Principles of Dr. James Frank".

Additional notes and reflections could be included in this chapter. The writer could add many positive comments people have shared with her down through the years. The additions would be numerous enough to compile another separate book.

On a quiet and sunny Sunday evening around 6:00 p. m. July 8, 2018, while conversing and enjoying time at their lake house, in

Lake Ozark, Missouri, the writer posed the following question to Dr. Frank: "What would you say is responsible for the tremendous amount of success you have experienced?" His quick and spontaneous response was "God! I took advantage of opportunities, I knew nothing would just happen, and I was fortunate to have met the right people at the right time."

On another occasion, during an interview for a local newspaper in Dallas, Texas, he was asked about the keys to his success and his becoming the first Black president of the NCAA. His response was as follows:

I managed to stay healthy, and I believe in the goodness of people, hard work, and being a good human being. It has been an honor and blessing to serve and be involved in such a prestigious and influential organization as the NCAA.

- Article in the *Dallas Examiner*,
April 3, 2014, written by Diane Xavier.

He accepted an invitation to attend the annual meeting of the National Association of Collegiate Directors of Athletics (NACDA) to share his views on some of the current issues in college sports and his historical climb to the position of president Directors of the NCAA. That took place on June 13, 2016. The NACDA president made it clear that he did not need to prepare a formal presentation. The NACDA president just wanted him to share his knowledge and wisdom in an informal setting. That request speaks volumes about

Dr. James Frank's influence in the world of sports and education. His record speaks for itself.

Finally, a birthday message from his wife, dated October 6, 2017, is certainly a tribute and reads as follows:

Dear Jim,

You are so special and remain so even after fifty-nine years of marriage. You, having been born in Aliquippa, Pennsylvania, and me in Kansas City, Missouri, I thank God that our paths merged in 1957 at Lincoln University in Jefferson City, Missouri. Since our marriage in 1958, you have been my lifelong partner and best friend, so I say, "Thanks." Thanks also for the memories, and for keeping your promise to "show me the world" if I married you. Our life has been nothing less than spectacular!

I love you, Jim,

Happy Birthday!

Zelma

Chapter 13

The Legacy Continues

If you're going to live, leave a legacy. Make a mark on the world that can't be erased.
Maya Angelou

Dr. Frank speaking at a convocation on the Lincoln University Campus circa 1980. (Photograph by Lincoln University)

D r. James Frank's journey is far from over. It is now in a season of continuation. Legacy is the impact one has had on people, organizations, or institutions that continues to benefit those entities in perpetuity. In the simplest terms, according to Webster's Dictionary, a legacy is "something transmitted by or received from an ancestor or predecessor or from the past." Whether the legacy is something material or intangible, it is passed on to subsequent generations for their benefit.

Through *Seasons of the Journey*, the author has well documented the legacies Dr. Frank transmitted to the world throughout his life – legacies which exemplify integrity, professionalism, educational excellence, hard-work ethics, athletic endeavor, unselfishness, and family values. Dr. Frank held many prominent positions. His leadership skills and accomplishments were exemplary and indelible. He touched the lives of many. He was thoroughly recognized throughout his life for his impact. He had an impactful influence on many universities and organizations, two of which were Lincoln University and the Southwestern Athletic Conference (SWAC), where significant edifices will now bear his name.

The executive leadership of both Lincoln University and the Southwestern Athletic Conference have chosen to further his legacy. Founders Hall on the Lincoln University campus was renamed Dr. James Frank Hall on April 21, 2023. The Southwestern Athletic Conference national headquarters building in Birmingham, Alabama, has been named in his honor. The official naming ceremony has been scheduled to take place on October 26, 2023. His name on these important and historical edifices cements his legacy and his significant impact on these two great entities.

LINCOLN UNIVERSITY
The Newly Renamed Frank Hall

The newly named Frank Hall (formerly Founders Hall) on the University quadrangle (the Quad) next to the new Memorial Hall, Young Hall, and the Soldier's Memorial that includes two bronze soldier statues on the sidewalk, taking the journey from war to education and beyond. Frank Hall is diagonally across from Schweich Hall (not shown) and directly across the quadrangle from Stamper Hall (not shown). (Photograph by Trent Frank, 4/21/23)

Frank Hall renaming ceremony

April 21, 2023, Lincoln University, Jefferson City, Missouri

On Tuesday, April 21, 2023, at an outdoor ceremony on the campus of Lincoln University, the renaming of Founders Hall to Dr. James Frank Hall took place. Frank Hall, a large building, is in a prominent location on the quadrangle along with Memorial Hall, Young Hall, Schweich Hall, and Stamper Hall. It is also in proximity to the magnificent, expansive, bronze Soldier's Memorial sculpture. The location of Frank Hall in relation to the other buildings and the soldier's memorial is significant. Dr. Frank's name is in Memorial

Hall as a distinguished alumnus, and he initiated the fundraising for that building; his office was located in Young Hall; Schweich Hall is where he and his wife began their lifelong relationship and where his younger son, years later, attended preschool; and Stamper Hall is named after one of his former employees, and also where his son, Dr. Troy Frank, currently teaches and has an office location. The above circumstances make this a storied honor.

Some members of Dr. James Frank's family listened to remarks at the Frank Hall Renaming Ceremony with additional family and friends in the background. From left to right, Zelma Frank, Troy Frank, Trent Frank, Albert Frank, Rosetta (Frank) Screven, and Earl Screven (Photograph by Lincoln University, 4/21/23)

It was a sunny and very windy day in Jefferson City, Missouri. People from the community were there to witness the historic occasion. Numerous relatives and friends were in attendance, many of whom had traveled great distances to be there. Dr. Frank's two sons, Trent and Troy, his grandchildren, Tracia and Simeon, his brother, Albert Frank, his sister, Rozetta Screven, her husband, Earl, and three generations of nieces and nephews, several of whom graduated from Lincoln while Dr. Frank was president, were among the numerous relatives who were present. The huge turnout exemplified much love and respect for Dr. Frank.

Dr. John Moseley, President of Lincoln University, presented the opening remarks at the Frank Building before a large audience of supporters in front of the building on the University Quadrangle (the Quad). (Photograph by Lincoln University, 4/21/23)

The program participants spoke about Dr. Frank's influence, legacy, and contributions to Lincoln University and beyond. Dr. John Moseley, Lincoln University president, said

"Good morning, and welcome home to Lincoln University. I say welcome home because I understand that while the Frank family had mailing addresses in different parts of the country, Lincoln University was always home for Dr. James Frank from his first days on campus in 1949 until his last visit. One thing was abundantly clear; he loved this University.

Today is a big day for our university and for me personally. Serving in the role in which I now serve, I've heard the whispers of, 'What does a basketball coach know about being president?' Well, I think Dr. Frank has already answered that one for us.

No matter where his career took him, his mind and his work somehow always managed to be right here with us. Even in retirement, his commitment to Lincoln was beyond financial, although he left a mark in that way as well.

I believe today's renaming is a fitting tribute to a man whose life was a testimony to what it means to be a true Lincolnite. Our University Oath reminds us to leave Lincoln better than it was when we arrived. Every time Dr. James Frank stepped on this campus, he made it better, and this renaming is in celebration of that."

Mr. Victor Pasley, President of the Board of Curators, presented laudatory remarks before an audience of supporters in front of the building on the University Quadrangle. (Photograph by Lincoln University, 4/21/23)

Mr. Victor Pasley, President of the Board of Curators and leader of the renaming initiative, made the following remarks,

"It is my honor, as president of the Board of Curators, to welcome you here for this special occasion. Today, we recognize a man whose Lincoln University history bears a unique distinction. In 1949, James Frank started his Lincoln experience, as many of our Blue Tiger students do today-with the acceptance of a scholarship. That basketball scholarship paved the way for his Lincoln education – he graduated with honors in 1953 – and the start of an incredible lifetime of achievement and dedication to Lincoln University. The Board of Curators' action to rename Founders Hall to Dr. James Frank Hall reflects the impact that Dr. Frank had and that he continues to have.

"In 1973, Dr. Frank became the only Lincoln University alumnus to be selected as president of this great institution. Adding to his significance, after his tenure was over, he continued to support and serve as a champion for the University. Beyond his service to Lincoln, he was also a highly respected leader on a national level.

"While still serving as president of Lincoln, Dr. Frank was elected president of the NCAA, the only African American and first college president in that post. This achievement brought prestige to Lincoln University, HBCUs, and all NCAA Division II schools. He was also appointed Southwestern Athletic Conference Commissioner (SWAC), again boosting national recognition of HBCUs and encouraging inclusiveness.

"After his tenure as LU president, Dr. Frank continued to serve through the Lincoln University Foundation, particularly through fundraising. For example, he led the charge to pay off a seven hundred-fifty-thousand-dollar shortfall to complete the two-million-dollar Soldier's Memorial, and when Lincoln tore down Memorial Hall and built a new one, Dr. Frank drove the fundraising for that project. Over the course of his life, he contributed over three hundred thousand dollars to Lincoln in personal gifts.

"He was a ten-time Hall of Fame honoree. He was an army officer and veteran, a professor, a basketball coach, an academic dean, and a scholar. He was a husband and father. This Lincoln University alumnus and president held many titles and impacted so many lives. Today, his legacy lives on."

*Rev. Trent Frank presented remarks at the Frank Building Renaming Ceremony in front of the building on the University Quadrangle.
(Photograph by Lincoln University, 4/21/23)*

Dr. Frank's son, Trent, talked about all the examples his father had set for him through his observations of his father's life of leadership, scholarship, dedication, and unselfishness in helping others. He spoke about how impactful this influence was during his childhood as he grew up in White Plains, New York, and Jefferson City, Missouri, and then into adulthood. Witnessing his father's accomplishments and essential leadership roles shaped his own philosophy about how to be a caring and effective leader. He stated that those examples also served as a primary reason he felt the renaming of Founders Hall was well-deserved.

Dr. Troy Frank presented remarks at the Frank Building Renaming Ceremony in front of the building on the University Quadrangle. (Photograph by Lincoln University, 4/21/23)

Dr. Frank's younger son, Troy, spoke about his father's influence on his life, goals, and career choices. He reflected on the many trips he took with his father and how he learned so much about life, education, sports, and leadership while sitting at his side. He cited examples of the impact of his father's leadership roles in education and sports. He described his early childhood days growing up on the Lincoln University campus and the memorable times he spent in his father's office, not too far from where his own office is located today on the Lincoln campus. He read a poem he had written, which embodied a detailed chronological description of his father's life.

Dr. Zelma Frank presented the final remarks at the Frank Building Renaming Ceremony before an audience of supporters in front of the building on the University Quadrangle. (Photograph by Lincoln University, 4/21/23)

Mrs. Frank thanked the president of the University, the president of the Board of Curators, and the members of the board for renaming Founders Hall in honor of her husband. Several board members were present. Vernon Bracy, Stacia Bradley Brown, and Terry Rackers attended. Mrs. Frank also thanked family and friends for their attendance. She discussed how they first met on the campus in 1957, pointing to the building, Schweich Hall, where he initiated their walk to Bennett Hall, the senior girl's dormitory. She called it the historic walk and the beginning of a love story.

She spoke of feeling his presence as she made reference to many of his legacies on campus, some of which were evidenced within view as she spoke – his name on a plaque leading to the Soldier's Memorial, his name on bricks and a paver around the memorial, Young Hall where his office was located, and Memorial Hall where he is listed as a Distinguished Alumnus. She went on to say that his picture is in Page Library along with other former presidents, his name is on one wing of the Wellness Center, and he is listed in the ROTC Building as a Lincoln University ROTC Hall of Fame inductee.

She revealed a copy of his biography, which will be published and available for sale beginning in the summer of 2023. Mrs. Frank stated that his biography would enable others to also feel his presence on the Lincoln University campus. A portion of the proceeds from "Seasons of the Journey: The Biography of Dr. James Frank" will be used to further fund the scholarships at Lincoln University, which are in Dr. Frank's name. Mrs. Frank spoke proudly of her husband's character and his many accomplishments.

She further stated that his life exemplified two quotes, "Do not follow where the path may lead, go instead where there is no path, and leave a trail," Ralph Waldo Emerson, and "Life is not important except in the impact it has on other lives." Jackie Robinson. Dr. Frank's accomplishments were innovative and had an impact on the lives of many.

Missouri State Representative Michael Johnson presented Mrs. Zelma Frank
with a Resolution by the Missouri House of Representatives in
recognition of the building dedication and tribute to Dr. Frank
(Photograph by Lincoln University, 4/12/23)

Mr. Michael Johnson, Missouri State Representative, District 23, and vice chair of the Missouri Black Caucus presented a Resolution to Mrs. Frank. The wording in the proclamation was a fitting historical summary of Dr. Frank's life accomplishments and his numerous and unique contributions to Lincoln University and the nation. The Missouri House of Representatives recognized the dedication of Dr. James Frank Hall and paid "tribute to Dr. Frank, a remarkable gentleman whose unwavering commitment to education and collegiate sports continues to serve as an inspiration to all of those who knew and loved him." It was an awesome occasion for an alumnus and former Lincoln University President so deserving of the honor.

Members of Drs. James and Zelma Frank's family posed after the renaming ceremony. Included in the picture are great nieces and nephews, as well as nieces who attended or graduated from Lincoln during Dr. Frank's Tenure. (Photograph by Daphney Frank Elder)

Members of Dr. Frank's proud Alpha-Phi-Alpha Fraternity were present at the Frank building renaming ceremony as a show of support and recognition. Seated at the center are Dr. Arnold Parks, Professor Emeritus (l), and Mr. Victor Pasley, President, Lincoln University Board of Curators (r).

Another view of the expansive newly named Frank Hall (right), formerly Founders Hall, on the University quadrangle next to the new Memorial Hall, Young Hall, and the Soldier's Monument that includes two bronze soldier statues on the sidewalk taking the journey from war to education and beyond. (Photograph by Trent Frank, 4/21/23)

SOUTHWESTERN ATHLETIC CONFERENCE (SWAC)

Headquarters Building Named in honor of Dr. James Frank

The newly named Southwestern Athletic Conference (SWAC) corporate office building is located near downtown Birmingham, AL. (Photograph by SWAC)

SWAC Announced Naming of Headquarters Building

The Southwestern Athletic Conference (SWAC) Council of Presidents and Chancellors* voted unanimously to accept the SWAC Commissioner's proposal to name the conference headquarters building in honor of Dr. James Frank. Dr. Frank was the first full-time commissioner of the conference and established the first conference office, which he negotiated to have located in the New Orleans Super Dome. He oversaw SWAC's unprecedented growth in funding, sponsorships, and popularity. Dr. Frank established a SWAC scholarship in his name, which enables student athletes to pursue Master's Degrees in Physical Education or related fields.

The SWAC website description of the headquarters building reads as follows: "… 16,000 square feet corporate office building located near downtown Birmingham. The three-story structure is equipped with over 40 individual offices, two large conference rooms, a walk-in reception/waiting area, and over 30 parking spaces. The league's new headquarters will fittingly serve as the primary location for conference operations and annual business meetings, along with the onsite filming of multimedia content for distribution via social media and the SWAC Digital Network (SDN)."

On June 27, 2023, under the leadership of the current SWAC Commissioner, Dr. Charles McClelland, the SWAC office issued the following press release:

> "The Southwestern Athletic Conference Council of Presidents and Chancellors has announced the naming of the building that currently serves as the headquarters for league operations.

> "The conference office headquarters located in Birmingham, Alabama, has officially been named the "Dr. James Frank Building" in honor and recognition of Dr. James Frank, who served as SWAC Commissioner from 1983-1998.

> "Dr. Frank's impact and legacy with the NCAA and the Southwestern Athletic Conference is truly remarkable," said SWAC Commissioner Dr. Charles McClelland. "He was a true pioneer in the field of collegiate athletics, and his vision and legacy continue to positively impact countless student athletes, both past and present.

> "The Southwestern Athletic Conference will forever be indebted to Dr. Frank and his contributions to our league. The naming of our conference headquarters in his honor is truly fitting

and undoubtedly well-deserved as we look to continually honor the historic contributions he made that have helped shape our conference into what it is today.

"During Dr. Frank's presidency, he was a significant influence in defining NCAA decisions:

- Dr. Frank chaired the governance subcommittee and oversaw the governance plan that defined how and when women's sports and championships would become part of the NCAA.

- He presided over the passing of Proposition 48, the legislation that set eligibility standards for incoming freshman student-athletes, which resulted in raising graduation rates.

- Dr. Frank facilitated enhanced presidential collaboration through the NCAA Long-Range Planning Committee, which led to a demographic change in Association leadership.

- He was integral in the NCAA's establishment of the Minority Opportunities and Interest Committee, a group devoted to inclusiveness in Association policy decisions.

"From 1983 until his retirement in 1998, Dr. Frank served as Commissioner of the Southwestern Athletic Conference (SWAC). He returned to the position as Interim Commissioner in April 2001, where he served for 20 months. During his guidance, the conference evolved to rank among the elite in the nation.

"During Dr. Frank's tenure as SWAC Commissioner, he was credited with:

- Providing stable leadership during the conference's early years as an NCAA Division I member.

- Spearheading conference expansion with the additions of Alabama State, Alabama A&M, and Arkansas-Pine Bluff as new members.

- Placing emphasis on gender equity and diversity by highlighting and expanding women's sports sponsorship during his tenure.

- Operating the Conference Office in a financially prudent manner during his tenure.

"Dr. James Frank was one of a few individuals who elevated through the collegiate ranks as a student-athlete, coach, educator, college president, and conference commissioner. During a long and distinguished career of over 50 years, Frank's efforts and influential leadership touched the lives of countless people and resulted in positive changes in the many organizations he served.

"A formal ceremony recognizing the naming of the league's headquarters in honor of Dr. Frank will be held at a later date."

Subsequent to the above press release, Commissioner McClelland set the date of the official naming ceremony for October 26, 2023, in Birmingham, Alabama, during the weekend of the popular Magic City Classic, the annual football game between SWAC universities Alabama State and Alabama A&M.

A complete list of Dr. Frank's many achievements and contributions to the conference can be found in Chapter Nine of this biography. He was a brilliant leader and trailblazer. His life epitomized the theme of his SWAC retirement celebration, "A Man for All Seasons." He was indeed an American icon.

*The SWAC Council of Presidents and Chancellors as of this writing:

Dr. Andrew Hugine, President, Alabama A & M

Dr. Quinton T. Ross, President, Alabama State

Dr. William Berry, Interim President, Bethune Cookman

Dr. Larry Robinson, President, Florida A & M

Dr. Elayne Hayes Anthony, Interim President, Jackson State

Dr. Jerryl Briggs, Sr., President, Mississippi Valley

Dr. Tracy Cook, Interim President, Alcorn State

Dr. Lawrence B. Alexander, Chancellor, University of Arkansas at Pine Bluff

Dr. Richard J. Gallot, Jr., President, Grambling State

Dr. Tomika P. Le Grande, President, Prairie View A & M

Dr. Dennis J. Shields, President-Chancellor, Southern University

Dr. Mary Evans, Interim President, Texas Southern

*At the time the voting took place, Dr. Lesia Crumpton-Young was president of Texas Southern, and Dr. Daniel Wims was president of Alabama A & M.

Chapter 14

In Poetic Memory

"James Frank loved the game of golf. On January 24, 2019, he quietly and peacefully strolled off of life's 18th Green after sinking a miraculous 88-foot (age) putt. With his signature smile and gentle, unassuming demeanor, he waved to the gallery and wished us all farewell before heading into the Lord's clubhouse to calculate a near-perfect scorecard."
Troy Frank

In honor of Doctor Frank and his love of literature, this chapter is affectionately and appropriately titled, "In Poetic Memory."

The writer has included the following poem, written by Dr. Frank's son, Dr. Troy Frank, to symbolize familial sentiments regarding Dr. Frank. Troy shared the poem during the Gerald R. Ford Award presentation.

**Testimony To A Good Man
Dr. James Frank**

By Dr. Troy Frank

Father, Coach, Leader, and Guide
Athlete, Teacher, and source of pride
Your face displays the trademark smile.
Which makes one want to stay awhile

Your upbringing in a steel mill town
Has grounded you well for the success you've found.

A life filled with sacrifice, dedication, and some pain
Has paved your way and has been your gain.

Determined and focused, you knew what had to be done
You've worked hard and smart to achieve better for your sons.

Late nights and endless days
We've watched you work through life's every phase.

Your commitment and drive were, at times, hard to understand,
But as we look back, we see that God had a plan;

A plan that would impact the lives of family;
A life of character, discipline, and integrity.

Your life exemplifies all that we believe
Humility and hard work breed an honor that not all achieve.

Now it's a new day with a grandchild peering at you
A bright-eyed little girl who loves you through and through.

We know you will embrace this life with the same zeal and power
Your life will be a testimony of truth to this dear little flower.

Words truly can't express the power you possess.
By living a life of truth, you've given us all YOUR best.

With Much Love, Troy, Trent, Pamela, and Tracia

**The poem was written before Trent's second child, Simeon, was born; therefore, his name does not appear in the close.*

Dr. Frank has always been a Bridge Builder, wanting to make things better for those who would come after him. That is why he so strongly connects to the Lincoln University Oath, quoted earlier in this biography, and reads in part," …. We will transmit our University to those who come after us, greater, better, and more beautiful than it was transmitted to us." This philosophy and his journey have positively affected the lives of many. The writer believes that the following poem epitomizes his philosophical view of what he felt was a part of his purpose on earth.

The Bridge Builder

An old man going on a lone highway
Came at the evening cold and gray
To a chasm vast and deep and wide.
The old man crossed in the twilight dim.
The sullen stream had no fears for him.
But he turned when safe on the other side.
And built a bridge to span the tide.

"Old man," said a pilgrim near,
"You are wasting your strength building here;
Your journey will end at the ending day,
You never again will pass this way;
You've crossed the chasm deep and wide,
Why build this bridge at evening tide?"

The builder lifted his old gray head –
"Good friend, in the path I have come," he said,
"There followeth after me today
A youth whose feet must pass this way,
This chasm that has been as naught to me
To that fair-headed youth may a pitfall be,
He, too, must cross in the twilight dim,
Good friend, I am building this bridge for him."

-Anon

In 2017 when his niece, Dr. Stacia Bradley Brown, was giving a speech at a Lincoln University Foundation Scholarship luncheon, she ended it by reading the poem, "Power of One." The writer immediately thought about Dr. Frank and how that poem was so descriptive of his life, philosophy, and journey. That poem reads as follows:

Power Of One

Ashish Ram

One song can spark a moment,
One whisper can wake the dream.
One tree can start a forest,
One bird can herald spring.

One smile begins a friendship,
One moment can make one fall in Luv.
One star can guide a ship at sea,
One word can frame the goal.

One vote can change a nation,
One sunbeam lights a room.
One candle wipes out darkness,
One laugh will conquer gloom.

One step must start each journey.
One word must start each prayer.
One hope will raise our spirits,
One touch can show you care.
One voice can speak with wisdom,
One heart can know what's true,
One life can make a difference,
You see, it's up to you!

While he received many awards during his life journey, he also made many friends. He always had favorite quotes and poems. One of his long-time favorite books in that genre was destroyed during Hurricane Katrina in August 2005, when he and his family lived in New Orleans, Louisiana. He had reflected on many of his favorites in retirement, some of which were in that lost book. One of those poems, in particular, resonated with the writer as she reflected on his retirement years, his many friends and acquaintances scattered throughout the United States, and how he kept in touch with so many of them. The poem, which was one of Dr. Frank's favorites, is titled "Around the Corner."

Around The Corner

Charles Hanson Towne

Around the corner, I have a friend,
In this great city that has no end,
Yet the days go by, and weeks rush on,
And before I know it, a year is gone.

I never see my old friend's face,
For life is a swift and terrible race,
He knows I like him just as well,
As in the days when I rang his bell.

And he rang mine, but we were younger then,
And now we are busy, tired men.
Tired of playing a foolish game,
Tired of trying to make a name.
"Tomorrow," I say! "I will call on Jim
Just to show that I'm thinking of him."
But tomorrow comes and tomorrow goes,
And the distance between us grows and grows.

Around the corner, yet miles away,
"Here's a telegram, sir, "Jim died today."

And that's what we get and deserve in the end.
Around the corner, a vanished friend.

Dr. Frank often used poetry and quotes in his speeches. In the Lincoln University Commencement Speech on May 15, 1976, he challenged the graduates by saying,

"I pray that the knowledge and experience you have gained here will help prepare you for your life's work. As you go forth, I ask you to carry the message of this poem with you."

I Shall Not Pass This Way Again
(Anonymous)

Through this toilsome world, alas!
    Once and only once I pass,
    If a kindness I may show,
    If a good deed I may do
    To a suffering fellow man,
    Let me do it while I can.
    No delay, for it is plain
    I shall not pass this way again.

Dr. Frank's love of poetry began during his youth and continued throughout his life.

Concluding Notes

from

DRS. JAMES and ZELMA FRANK

Drs. James and Zelma Frank were at a friend's house in Los Angeles, California. During that time, they were in Los Angeles for Dr. Frank to receive the Black Chamber of Orange County 2008 Aaron-Elijah Lovejoy Award.

From Dr. James Frank

I approve of the content and clarity of this biography and the intent, integrity, and honesty of the writer. And, to the writer, I say Thanks. I am very appreciative. Thanks to you, the reader, for joining me on my journey by reading this manuscript. I pray for God's blessings upon you as you continue your journey through life.

From Dr. Zelma Lloyd Frank

Writing Dr. James Frank's biography has been one of the most enjoyable projects the writer has ever undertaken. She is grateful for the opportunity to have written this biography and to share it with you, the reader. May Dr. Frank's journey continue to be a beacon of light whose radiance all can see. I hope his story will motivate other young people to be the best they can be and merit the recording of their histories. He chose the path of success rather than failure.

Never to be minimized is the fact that when he was in high school, his counselor enrolled him in the industrial curriculum rather than the academic curriculum assuming that, because of his poverty he would not be going to college. This was to ignore his intellect, athletic ability, and scholarship possibilities. What would have happened had he chosen to traverse the path that someone else had carved out for him? Indeed, that biography, if even written, would have read differently.

The line from "Invictus, "I am the master of my fate," has relevancy in this biographical journey. So, in summary, that poem is an appropriate ending for this historical recording of Dr. Frank's journey. It was also one of his favorites, and one he was required to memorize during his initiation into Alpha Phi Alpha Fraternity.

Invictus

William Ernest Henley

Out of the night that covers me,

Black as the Pit from pole to pole,

I thank whatever gods may be

For my unconquerable soul.

In the fell clutch of circumstance

I have not winced nor cried aloud.

Under the bludgeoning of chance

My head is bloody but unbowed.

Beyond this place of wrath and tears

Looms but the horror of the shade,

And yet the menace of the years.

Finds, and shall find me unafraid.

It matters not how strait the gate,

How charged with punishment the scroll

I am the master of my fate,

I am the captain of my soul.

The writing of this biography represents a labor of love in tribute to the writer's husband, Dr. James Frank, a trailblazer, leader, and legend - A Man for all Seasons. To use the motto for the National Baseball Hall of Fame, this biography has also been written for the purpose of "Preserving History, Honoring Excellence, Connecting Generations."   The writer thanks you, the reader, for traveling with her through the seasons of Dr. James Frank's journey.

About The Author

Drs. James and Zelma Frank

Dr. Zelma Lloyd Frank is a retired educator with bachelor's and master's degrees from Lincoln University (Mo.), a master's degree from Herbert H. Lehman College of the City University of New York, and a doctorate from the University of Missouri, Columbia. Her career has included the following: teaching in elementary schools in Kansas, Missouri, Massachusetts, and New York; reading consultant and diagnostician in elementary and junior high schools in White Plains, New York; teaching methodology courses in education at Hunter College, the City University of New York; instructor and director of the reading clinic at Lincoln

University (Missouri); English professor and director of student support services at Southern University in New Orleans, Louisiana.

She has conducted workshops and seminars for college personnel on teaching strategies and services for students with disabilities and has been a certified instructional trainer for the Association on Higher Education and Disability. Dr. Zelma Frank worked with the United States Department of Education as an evaluator of federally funded education programs (TRIO) and served as a consultant to the Missouri Department of Education.

She has written articles on curriculum and instruction which have been published in journals of higher education and is the author of *The History of the President's Houses at Lincoln University*. Her doctoral dissertation, "The Portrayal of Black Americans in Pictures and Content in the Caldecott Award Books and Honor Books from 1938 to 1978," has been replicated. The dissertation highlights the sparsity of African Americans in children's books and details the need for children to see people who look like them in the books they read.

Dr. Frank has received the following honors and awards: special recognition for having written and received federal funding for six consecutive Student Support Services proposals; first female graduation Marshall at Southern University in New Orleans; marshall for the graduates when receiving her doctorate from the University of Missouri; featured in a Lincoln University library display that highlighted women who have made historical contributions to the University; inducted into the Lincoln University Alumni Hall of Fame; received the Kansas City, Missouri Lincoln

High School Alumni Award for Outstanding Achievement; and the Women as Winners YWCA of Greater New Orleans Award for personal and professional achievement and being a role model and mentor for young girls and other women. Dr. Frank is a "Pearl" Life Member of Alpha Kappa Alpha Sorority, Inc. She was married to Dr. James Frank for sixty years.

She was married to Dr. James Frank for sixty years and has two sons and two grandchildren.

List of Footnotes

Chapter 1

1. S.L. Price, *Playing Through the Whistle: Steel, Football, and an American town* (New York, Atlantic Monthly Press, 2016), 9.

2. Price, Playing, p. 8.

3. "Black Steelworkers in Western Pennsylvania," Pennsylvania Heritage, last modified December 1977, https://www.paheritage.wpengine.com/article/black-steelworkers-western-pennsylvania/

4. Price, Playing, 24

5. Price, Playing, 99

Chapter 2

6. Mike Ditka, *An Autobiography* (Chicago, Bonus Books, Inc., 1986)

Chapter 3

7. Ebony Magazine, Article Title, and Date Unknown

Chapter 6

8. Source: Multiple public sources, Lincoln Archives, and Lincoln University Atlanta Alumni Chapter Founder's Day Program. 2011.

9. Phone conversations between 2019-2020

10. Obtained from Lincoln University Archivist, Mark Schleer, 2018

Chapter 7

11. Atlanta Journal Constitution, Nov. 8, 2021

12. Joe Crowley, *In the Arena: The NCAA's First Century* (Indianapolis, NCAA, 2005)

13. "Growth," NCAA, Accessed March 1, 2022, https://www.ncaa.org/sports/2021/5/4/history.aspx:

14. "Growth," NCAA, Accessed March 1, 2022, https://www.ncaa.org/sports/2021/5/4/history.aspx:

15. Crowley, Arena, iii

16. Crowley, Arena, iv

17. Crowley, *Arena,* iv

18. Crowley, Arena, iv

19. Crowley, Arena, 65

20. Crowley, Arena, 131

21. "Growth," NCAA, Accessed March 1, 2022, https://www.ncaa.org/sports/2021/5/4/history.aspx:

22. "Growth," NCAA, Accessed March 1, 2022, https://www.ncaa.org/sports/2021/5/4/history.aspx:

23. Crowley, Arena, 131

24. First Black NCAA President, Dr. James Frank has Died," HBCU Buzz Reporters, Last Modified January 28, 2019 - https://hbcubuzz.com/2019/01/first-black-ncaa-president-dr-james-frank-has-died/.

25. From Myles Brand speech during Gerald R. Ford Award ceremony on 1/12/2008

26. Crowley, Arena, v.

27. Lauren Kirschman, "Layup Decisions," Beaver County Times, March 13, 2016

Chapter 8

28. Written by Lincoln University Archivist, Mark Schleer for The James Frank Display at Inman E. Page Library, Lincoln University

29. Obtained from Lincoln University Archivist, Mark Schleer, 2018

Works Cited

Crowley, Joe. In The Arena: *The NCAA's First Century.*
Indianapolis: NCAA, 2005)

Ditka, Mike. *Ditka, An Autobiography.* Chicago: Bonus Books,
1986

Frank, Zelma. *A History of the House for Lincoln University
Presidents*, Jefferson City: Lincoln University Graphic
Arts, 1981

HBCU Buzz Reporters. "First Black NCAA President, Dr. James
Frank has Died." Last Modified January 28, 2019,
https://hbcubuzz.com/2019/01/first-black-ncaa-president-
dr-james-frank-has-died

Kirschman, Lauren. "Layup Decisions." Beaver County Times,
March 13, 2016

NCAA. "Growth." Accessed March 1, 2022,
https://www.ncaa.org/sports/2021/5/4/history.aspx:

Pennsylvania Heritage. *"Black Steelworkers in Western
Pennsylvania."* Last modified December 1977
Paheritage.wpengine.com/article/black-steelworkers-
western-Pennsylvania/

Price, S. L. *Playing Through the Whistle: Steel, Football, and an American Town*, New York: Atlantic Monthly Press, 2016.

Savage, Sherman. *History of Lincoln University*, Jefferson City: Lincoln University, 1940

Dr. James Frank's Publications

Frank, J., "The Problem of the Black Administrator." AGB Reports, January/February 1981.

Frank, J., "Status of Women's Intercollegiate Athletics by 1980: A Personal View." NCAA News, November 1980.

Frank, J., "Urban Physical Education" NYSAHPER Student Newsletter, Fall, 1968.

Frank. J., "International Relations Through Health, Physical Education and Recreation." NYSAHPER Journal, Spring 1968.

Frank, J., "Understanding Through International Relations." NYSAHPER Journal, Spring 1968.

Frank, J., and Lipton, Aaron, "Impeding School Integration: Solutions to Educational Problems." Integrated Education, May 1967.

Frank, J., "Elementary School - Not Too Early For Inter-Scholastic Sports." The Physical Educator, March 1965.

Frank, J., "The Relationship of Some Selected Socio-Economic Factors To Changes In Physical Education Programs In Certain Localities In Missouri." Doctoral Dissertation. June 1963

www.ingramcontent.com/pod-product-compliance
Lightning Source LLC
Chambersburg PA
CBHW041307120726

48005CB00014B/1903